BEYOND THE MYTH

A Critical Analysis of Misinformed Narratives About the Chakma and Hajong of Arunachal Pradesh Impacting Academia and Society

ARUNJIT CHAKMA

- **Dedication** -

This book, ***Beyond the Myth: A Critical Analysis of Misinformed Narratives about Chakma and Hajongs of Arunachal Impacting Academia and Society***, is dedicated to you—the researchers, scholars, and thinkers of academia—whose relentless pursuit of knowledge lights the path toward a more just world. It is also for you—the citizens, students, and policymakers of society—whose hearts and hands can transform understanding into action. Together, you are the custodians of truth, the defenders of justice, and the voices capable of rewriting a narrative long marred by distortion and neglect.

For generations, the Chakma and Hajong communities of Arunachal Pradesh have borne the weight of myths and misrepresentations—cast as outsiders, refugees and illegal immigrants in a land they call home, their stories twisted by political agendas and buried under layers of indifference. Their scars tell a story of exclusion, yet their spirit speaks of resilience, a quiet courage that refuses to fade. This book is a call to you—to wield your pens, your intellect, and your compassion with unwavering purpose. It is an invitation to peel back the veil of misinformation and face the truths that demand to be seen, not out of pity, but as a duty to humanity.

To the scholars and researchers: Your work holds the power to pierce the shadows of ignorance. With every page you write, every question you ask, you can unravel the tangled history of the Chakma and Hajong, challenge the prejudices that have hardened over time, and lift up the voices that have been silenced. This dedication is a plea to harness that power—not just to seek knowledge, but to forge justice; not just to study the past, but to shape a future where truth reigns untainted by political expediency.

To society at large: This is your story too. To the students who dream of a better tomorrow, the citizens whose empathy can mend broken bonds, and the policymakers whose choices can right the wrongs of yesterday—the Chakma and Hajong are not mere footnotes in history. They are families, dreamers, and builders, their lives a testament to what happens when a nation turns its gaze away. Their journey is unfinished, and you hold the pen to write its next chapter—a conclusion worthy of the justice they deserve, rooted in the unshakable pillars of truth and humanity.

The scars of yesterday need not define tomorrow. This book is a spark, a call to action, a plea to rise above the forces of exclusion and craft a triumph of the human spirit. Let it ignite a movement where understanding triumphs over indifference, where justice prevails over convenience, and where the Chakma and Hajong find not just a voice, but a home in the conscience of a society that finally sees them for who they are.

With hope and unwavering resolve,

Arunjit Chakma

Contents

PREFACE

As a member of the Chakma community, born and raised in Arunachal Pradesh, I carry a history woven into the soil of this land—a history my family has lived and breathed for generations. Yet, too often, we are met with a piercing reminder: to many, we do not belong. The seeds of this book, *Beyond the Myth: A Critical Analysis of Misinformed Narratives About Chakma and Hajong Impacting Academia and Society*, were not sown in a moment of sudden clarity. They took root gradually, through a quiet, persistent unease that grew as I watched academics and researchers descend upon Diyun. They arrived with notebooks and recorders in hand, their minds alight with curiosity about the so-called "Chakma Refugee issue"—a phrase that, even in its utterance, felt like a cold, sterile label, far removed from the vibrant reality I call home.

It began with conversations—simple exchanges over steaming cups of chai, meant to bridge the chasm between their scholarly realm and the pulse of our daily lives. But what emerged instead was a troubling dissonance. It was as though they were reciting lines from a script penned by distant hands, a narrative that bore little trace of the truths I knew. Their questions, polished by academic rigor and shaped under professorial guidance, rang hollow, revealing a gulf of misunderstanding. Their research, bound by rigid frameworks, leaned on a foundation of outdated and biased literature. It was as if they gazed upon us through a warped lens, blind to the living, breathing complexity of our existence.

The source of this distortion was clear: their reliance on documents like the 1996 White Paper on the Chakma-Hajong issue—a text drenched in the state's perspective, wielded as an unassailable truth. These were not mere records of fact but political tools, sculpted to prop up a particular storyline. Absent from their pages were the voices of my people—the very souls they claimed to decipher. What emerged was a caricature of the Chakma, stripped down to faceless tags: "refugee," "illegal immigrant," "foreigner." These were not just missteps in language; they were deliberate reductions, as inaccurate as they were perilous.

The weight of this misrepresentation presses heavily upon us. We are not merely misunderstood—we are cast aside, vilified. These labels, unmoored from today's truths, have become weapons, wielded to rationalize our exclusion. We are painted as intruders, as threats to the tapestry of Arunachal Pradesh, despite roots that stretch deep into its earth. The pain of this is sharp and personal: to see our community smeared with such crude, dehumanizing strokes is to feel our very essence denied. These are not just words—they are chains, binding us to a false identity as perpetual outsiders in a place we've long called home.

This toxic narrative, birthed in the 1990s and fed by years of political and social fervour, clings stubbornly to the present. Its reach stretches far beyond the ivory towers of academia, seeping into societal perceptions, shaping policies, and fuelling discrimination. We are not specimens pinned under a microscope; we are people— individuals, families, communities—whose lives are scarred by these falsehoods.

This book is my stand against that tide of misinformation. It is a defiance of the labels—"refugee," "illegal immigrant," "foreigner"—that seek to define us. It is a plea for a richer, truer understanding of the Chakma story. More than that, it is a vow to lift up the voices that have been muted, to reclaim the narratives that have been twisted, and to shatter the myths that have clouded reality for too long. Through these pages, I seek not just to challenge the easy answers but to unearth the difficult truths—not with bitterness, but with an unshakable resolve to honour the lived experiences of my community, the Chakma people of Arunachal Pradesh, with clarity, empathy, and the firm belief that our stories matter.

Arunjit Chakma

ACKNOWLEDGEMENTS

In bringing *Beyond the Myth: A Critical Analysis of Misinformed Narratives About the Chakma and Hajong of Arunachal Pradesh Impacting Academia and Society* to fruition, I am deeply humbled by the collective spirit of the Chakma and Hajong communities. This book is more than a scholarly endeavour—it is a living narrative, born from the organic storytelling of our people. The need for such authentic voices, rooted in the lived experiences of our community, resonates with every member who has felt the weight of misrepresentation. For this, I am immensely grateful.

What sets this project apart is its unique foundation: it has been entirely crowdfunded by the members of our community. From the research to the publishing and printing, every step was made possible by the generous financial contributions of countless individuals who believed in the power of our story. The list of contributors is inexhaustible, and while I cannot name each one, I extend my heartfelt thanks to all who gave. Your support reflects the unyielding collective spirit that defines us, and it is the bedrock upon which this book stands.

This work is a testament to our shared resolve—to challenge misinformed narratives and to assert our truth. To everyone who has contributed, whether through resources, stories, or encouragement, I offer my deepest appreciation. Together, we have created something enduring—a record of our resilience, told in our own words, for our community and beyond.

With profound gratitude,

Arunjit Chakma

PROLOGUE

For decades, the discourse surrounding the Chakma and Hajong issue in Arunachal Pradesh has languished in the shadows of outdated and misleading narratives. The scarcity of contemporary, well-researched literature has allowed these myths to take root, perpetuating labels such as "refugee" and "stateless" that no longer align with the evolving socio-political reality. These narratives, mired in historical distortions, are not mere echoes of the past—they are living instruments of exclusion, warping the present-day truths of the Chakma and Hajong communities.

The need to unravel these myths transcends academic curiosity; it is a moral imperative. The persistent use of these labels is not a passive oversight—it is a deliberate act of erasure. It strips the Chakma and Hajongs of their rightful place within Arunachal Pradesh's socio-political tapestry, dismissing their resilience, their contributions, and their profound connection to the land. This is not just about setting the record straight; it is about reclaiming the dignity of Chakma & Hajong people who have endured systematic marginalization.

The 2024 elections cast a glaring spotlight on the fallacy of these outdated narratives. Over 9,400 Chakma and Hajong electors exercised their democratic right, casting votes that helped shape the political destiny of their state and nation. If they were truly "refugees," as some stubbornly assert, could they wield such a fundamental right? The question answers itself, laying bare the absurdity of these tired labels. Yet, their persistence hints at a darker truth: a calculated effort to suppress reality and preserve a narrative that benefits those who hold power.

This book unveils the "organic narrative"—a story not spun from political agendas but woven from the lived experiences of the Chakma and Hajong communities. It is a tale of perseverance against relentless odds, of vibrant cultural heritage, entrepreneurial spirit, and an unshakable sense of belonging. This narrative demands to be told not through the distant lens of outsiders but from the heart of the community itself. To achieve this, we must break free from the shackles of obsolete literature and embrace the authentic voices of the Chakma and Hajong. We must listen to their stories, honor their contributions, and weave their perspectives into the broader discourse. This shift is not just about factual precision—it is about transforming how these communities are seen and understood.

The Battle Against Narrative Suppression

I am no impartial bystander. I am a witness, fiercely committed to the truth. I have watched as deliberate efforts unfold to silence the authentic stories of the Chakma and Hajong people. From the political rhetoric that brands us "refugees" during election seasons to the overt stifling of our voices in academic spaces, the campaign to control this narrative is unmistakable. There exists a deeply entrenched system of misinformation, engineered to uphold a distorted storyline while burying the real one.

The evidence is undeniable. Politicians, especially during election campaigns, wield the "refugee" label as a weapon to marginalize the Chakma and Hajongs. Kiren Rijiju's rhetoric stands out as a stark example: he invokes this term while reaping the electoral support of the very people he seeks to delegitimize. This contradiction is not a slip—it is a strategic ploy to inflame divisions and garner votes through deception.

The events at Rajiv Gandhi University in 2024 offer a chilling glimpse into the lengths these forces will go to smother the truth. Professor Nani Bath's attempt to foster an academic dialogue—a "search for a democratic solution to the Chakma issue"—was met with fierce resistance from the All-Arunachal Pradesh Students' Union (AAPSU). Claiming sole authority over the "real story," the AAPSU sought to block the Chakma Panellist from speaking their own truth. This act of censorship, enacted within the sanctity of an academic institution, strikes at the core of intellectual freedom and the pursuit of knowledge. It exposes a broader agenda: to dominate the narrative at any cost.

This is not a solitary occurrence but part of a systematic pattern—a concerted strategy to extinguish the "organic narrative" of the Chakma and Hajong people. Groups like the AAPSU, alongside certain state actors, collaborate to mold public perception and policy, ensuring these communities remain on the periphery. They aim to erase our contributions, mute our voices, and perpetuate a story that serves their own ends.

This book is a counterstrike—a bold defiance of this machinery of suppression. It is more than an academic endeavour; it is an act of resistance, a cry for justice, and a call for recognition. By dissecting these misinformed narratives and laying bare the calculated attempts to manipulate discourse, this work seeks to forge a truer, more balanced understanding of the Chakma and Hajong communities. The ultimate aim is not merely to reclaim our story but to chart a path toward a future where their dignity and rights are fully embraced.

In the pages ahead, I beckon you to stand with me in this struggle against narrative suppression. Let us dismantle the myths, amplify the silenced voices, and construct a discourse grounded in truth, compassion, and equity. The moment for transformation is upon us—let us seize it with unwavering resolve.

Arunjit Chakma

BEYOND THE LABEL: RE-EVALUATING THE STATUS OF THE CHAKMA AND HAJONGS OF ARUNACHAL PRADESH

Are the Chakma and Hajongs of Arunachal Refugees?

The question of whether the Chakma and Hajongs of Arunachal Pradesh are refugees is far more than a matter of words—it is a struggle for identity, legitimacy, and a rightful place within India's intricate socio-political landscape. For over five decades, this question has lingered, clouded by misconceptions and tethered to outdated narratives that persist in academic circles and public imagination alike. Let us be clear from the outset: to label the Chakma and Hajongs as "refugees" today is to fundamentally misrepresent their reality. While the term may have once brushed against the edges of their historical experience, it now falls woefully short of capturing the depth of their journey or the permanence of their roots.

To understand why, we must first anchor ourselves in the globally accepted definition of a "refugee." The United Nations High Commissioner for Refugees (UNHCR) describes a refugee as an individual compelled to flee their homeland due to a "well-founded fear of being persecuted," seeking formal asylum in another country through a structured process that grants legal protection and aid [1]. This definition evokes images of temporality—tents, camps, and dependency—a transient state awaiting resolution through return or resettlement. Yet, the Chakma and Hajongs' story veers decisively

---

[1] *UNHCR, what is a refugee, https://www.unhcr.org/us/what-refugee*

away from this framework, rooted instead in a deliberate act of belonging within the nation they now call home.

In 1964, the Chakma and Hajongs crossed into India not as foreigners pleading for asylum but as people displaced by internal turmoil within the undivided Indian subcontinent. Unlike the Tibetans, who sought and received formal asylum from India as exiles from Chinese oppression, the Chakma and Hajongs did not navigate the conventional asylum pathway. Their migration was, in essence, a return home within India after 17 years of an unfortunate and arbitrary designation of their homeland as part of East Pakistan. Forced to migrate due to communal violence and the submergence of their land caused by the Kaptai Dam in present-day Bangladesh, they came under India's migration policies, were officially registered by the government, issued relief and rehabilitation certificates, and received initial support. But this was merely the beginning—not the entirety—of their story.

What followed was no fleeting refuge but a meticulously planned resettlement and rehabilitation. Between 1964 and 1969, the Government of India permanently rehabilitated the Chakma and Hajongs in the North-East Frontier Agency (NEFA), now Arunachal Pradesh. Each family received five acres of dense, unyielding forest—a challenging endowment that demanded transformation—and approximately Rs 4,200, a significant sum in the 1960s, to build homes and livelihoods. This was not the stopgap aid of a refugee camp; it was the foundation for a lasting existence. With bare hands and unbroken resolve, they cleared the wilderness, tamed the land, and sowed the seeds of a new life—a powerful act of permanence that defies the transient nature of "refugeehood."

A critical yet often ignored milestone punctuates their transition: once their rehabilitation was complete, the government discontinued their refugee allowances or temporary relief. This was not a minor administrative detail—it was a defining shift. The cessation of aid or relief signalled the end of their provisional status and the beginning of their integration as self-reliant residents, equal in rights and responsibilities to those around them [2]. In the state's eyes, they were no longer displaced persons; they were settlers, meant to stay.

A key official communication from the Ministry of Rehabilitation, dated February 12, 1981, addressed to the Arunachal Pradesh government, clarified this transition. The letter stated:

"The scheme for settlement of Chakma families in Arunachal Pradesh was originally formulated by the then N.E.F.A. Administration/State Government and was recommended by them for consideration of the Rehabilitation Ministry. These were accordingly sanctioned by the Ministry of Rehabilitation. After implementation of these schemes, the work relating to the settlement of Chakma families was normalized by the then N.E.F.A. Administration in April 1968, vide letter No. RR/5/68, dated 8th April 1968, issued to various Deputy Commissioners concerned. Consequently, these families are now a part and parcel of the local population, and if any additional facilities are to be provided for them, these may be provided by the State Government from its own resources.[3]"

Today, the Chakma and Hajongs are not huddled in camps, reliant on external charity and aid. They are landowners, taxpayers, and, voters—active contributors to Arunachal Pradesh's growth for over half a century. Yet, the "refugee" label clings to them like a stubborn ghost, diminishing their legal migration, their painstaking rehabilitation, and their undeniable integration. This misnomer carries weight beyond semantics—it wounds. As one Chakma elder

---

[2] *57 Years After India Gave Them Refuge, Former Refugees From East Pakistan Threatened By Indian Xenophobia | Article-14,* *https://www.article-14.com/post/57-years-after-india-gave-them-refuge-former-refugees-from-east-pakistan-threatened-by-indian-xenophobia-61f9f4b18da1f*

[3] *Ministry of Rehabilitation Letter No. 12/1/80-Desk.IV dated February 12, 1981, to the Govt. of Arunachal Pradesh (MHA File No. 13024/5/73 AP Vol. III), National Archives of India*

lamented, "We've built our homes, raised our children, and enriched this soil with our sweat. Yet they call us outsiders, as if our decades here are invisible." This is not just a misunderstanding; it is an erasure of their truth.

This chapter is not a passive rehashing of history—it is a demand for recognition. It challenges us to shed the reductive lens of "refugeehood" and see the Chakma and Hajongs as architects of resilience and belonging, woven into the fabric of Arunachal Pradesh. To cling to the label is to dishonour their journey; to release it is to affirm their reality. In the pages that follow, we will sharpen this argument through a comparative lens, examining the Chakma and Hajongs alongside other refugee groups—Tibetans, Afghans, Sri Lankans, and Burmese. This analysis will illuminate the stark contrasts: where Tibetans remain tied to an unresolved exile, Afghans and Sri Lankans seek temporary refuge from conflict, and Burmese linger in legal limbo, the Chakma and Hajongs stand apart, their presence sanctioned and their integration deliberate.

Why This Matters: This is not mere academic exercise—it is a reclamation of narrative. The Chakma and Hajongs' migration was not a desperate flight but a state-sponsored reset, their place in India not a privilege but a promise. By dissecting their legal status, societal contributions, and the intent behind their resettlement, we will dismantle the myth of their "refugeehood" and replace it with clarity.

Looking Ahead: Through this comparative journey, we will uncover the Chakma and Hajongs' distinct story—a tale of roots, not refuge. We will explore their historical migration, their recognized place within India's framework, and the socio-political realities that affirm their belonging. Let us move forward with open eyes and fearless inquiry, ready to honour the Chakma and Hajongs' voice and rewrite the story that has too long been misread.

1.1. LAND OWNERSHIP: CHAKMA & HAJONGS VS. TIBETAN REFUGEES

The narrative surrounding the Chakma and Hajong communities in Arunachal Pradesh often portrays them as refugees residing in camps or temporary settlements. This characterization, however, stands in stark contrast to the reality experienced by the Chakma and Hajong communities, particularly concerning their land ownership. Upon their arrival in the erstwhile North-East Frontier Agency (NEFA), now Arunachal Pradesh, the Chakma were granted land, a significant act that fundamentally distinguishes their situation from the typical understanding of refugees under both international and Indian law. This chapter aims to critically analyse and debunk the **"refugee camp"** myth by examining the legal definitions of refugees, the implications of land ownership, the historical context of the Chakma and Hajongs' resettlement, and a comparison with the experiences of Tibetan refugees in India. By focusing on the tangible reality of land ownership, this analysis will demonstrate that the Chakma and Hajongs are not transient refugees but rather an integrated community with established rights within the state.

The term **"refugee"** carries specific legal connotations under international law. The 1951 Refugee Convention, a cornerstone of international refugee protection, defines a refugee as an individual who fears persecution in their country of origin due to their race, religion, nationality, membership in a particular social group, or political opinion, and is unwilling or unable to return [1]. The United Nations High Commissioner for Refugees (UNHCR) also provides a broader definition, including those forced to flee war, violence, conflict, or other circumstances that severely disrupt public order [2]. While these definitions emphasize the element of forced displacement and the need for international protection, they inherently suggest a temporary state of refuge in a host country. The idea that individuals seeking such temporary protection would be granted permanent ownership of land in the host nation appears contradictory to the core principles of refugee status.

In the Indian context, the legal framework surrounding refugees is less defined. India is not a signatory to the 1951 Refugee Convention or its 1967 Protocol and lacks a specific national refugee law [4]. Instead, refugees are generally treated as foreigners under existing laws like the Foreigners Act, 1946 [5]. The Model National Law on Refugees in India defines a refugee based on a well-founded fear of persecution or displacement due to external aggression, human rights violations, or events disrupting public order [6]. Despite the absence of a dedicated law, India has historically dealt with refugee situations on a case-by-case basis [7]. This approach, however, generally does not extend the same ownership rights to property as are granted to citizens; even foreign nationals residing in India typically require prior approval from state governments to own property [8]. Given this legal landscape, the fact that the Chakma and Hajongs of Arunachal Pradesh possess land ownership rights signifies a unique and distinct situation that challenges their categorization as typical refugees.

The reality for the Chakma and Hajongs in Arunachal Pradesh presents a significant departure from the conventional refugee paradigm, primarily due to the systematic land allotment they received. Upon their arrival between 1964 and 1969, each Chakma and Hajong family was granted five acres of land as part of a "definite

---

[4] *Understanding the Indian Refugee Law Framework -*
https://nyaaya.org/guest-blog/understanding-the-indian-refugee-law-framework/
[5] *Refugees in India - Wikipedia,*
https://en.wikipedia.org/wiki/Refugees_in_India
[6] *Model National Law on Refugees - [2001] ISILYBIHRL 19,*
https://www.worldlii.org/int/journals/ISILYBIHRL/2001/19.html
[7] *India's Refugee Policy - Indian National Bar Association,*
https://www.indianbarassociation.org/indias-refugee-policy/
[8] *nluassam.ac.in,*
https://nluassam.ac.in/docs/Journals/NLUALR/Volume-7/Article%2011.pdf

plan of rehabilitation" initiated by the Government of India [9]. This was not a temporary arrangement or a conditional lease; it was a transfer of ownership governed by the state's revenue laws, granting the Chakma and Hajongs tangible rights to the land. Government records indicate that a total of 10,799 acres were allocated for their settlement across three districts [10]. Some accounts even suggest allotments ranging from 5 to 10 acres per family [11]. This substantial and formalized land distribution, carried out with the consent of the NEFA administration and local tribal chiefs [12], points towards a clear policy of permanent integration rather than temporary refuge. The scale and nature of this resettlement program, involving the conferment of ownership rights, strongly indicate that the Chakma and Hajongs' situation transcends the typical temporary assistance and accommodation provided to refugees seeking asylum.

To further understand the distinctiveness of the Chakma and Hajongs' situation, it is useful to compare their land rights and settlement patterns with those of another significant refugee group in India: the Tibetan refugees. While India has provided refuge and support to Tibetans who began arriving in 1959, their land tenure status is markedly different. Tibetan refugees are typically allotted land on lease, with agreements often signed by the Central Tibetan Relief Committee (CTRC) rather than individual families [13]. They face limitations on owning property in their own names and their

---

[9] *Chakma of Arunachal Pradesh – CRDO,*
https://crdo.chakma.in/Chakma-of-arunachal-pradesh/
[10] *Statelessness : A Study of Chakma Refugees of Arunachal Pradesh - SAS Publishers, https://www.saspublishers.com/article/4656/download/*
[11] *land use pattern and food security of stateless: profile of arunachal Chakma, https://www.worldwidejournals.com/indian-journal-of-applied-research-(IJAR)/recent_issues_pdf/2019/October/land-use-pattern-and-food-security-of-stateless-profile-of-arunachal-Chakma_October_2019_1571897281_9711789.pdf*
[12] *Chakma of Arunachal Pradesh – CRDO,*
https://crdo.chakma.in/Chakma-of-arunachal-pradesh/
[13] *The Tibetan Rehabilitation Policy, 2014. - Ministry of Home Affairs, https://www.mha.gov.in/sites/default/files/2022-08/FFR_ANNEXURE_A_17092019%5B1%5D.pdf*

settlements are often formalized and centrally administered. [14]. Although early Tibetan refugees received land on lease and housing, this privilege was not extended to later arrivals [15]. Government guidelines explicitly outline the lease document process through the CTRC for renewable 20-year periods [16]. This comparison highlights a fundamental difference in the legal and social standing of the two groups. The Chakma and Hajongs, with their individual land titles and integration into recognized villages, possess a level of rootedness and legal recognition concerning land that is generally not afforded to Tibetan refugees in India. This contrast suggests a different underlying intent and approach in the resettlement policies for these two communities.

The Indian state's actions further underscore the recognition of the Chakma and Hajongs' land rights in Arunachal Pradesh. The initial land allotment in NEFA during the 1960s, despite the region's protected status under the Bengal Eastern Frontier Regulation of 1873 which restricts land acquisition by non-natives without government sanction [17], demonstrates a deliberate policy decision to facilitate their settlement and rehabilitation. More significantly, the Indian government's acquisition of land from 156 Chakma families in Hollongi in 2018 for the construction of the Donyi Polo Green Field Airport under the Right to Fair Compensation and Transparency in Land Acquisition, Rehabilitation and Resettlement Act, 2013 (LARR Act 2013)

---

[14] *Chakma, Hajongs in Arunachal Pradesh Face 'Uncertain Future' l*, *https://www.smalegal.in/home/the-stateless-status-of-tibetans-in-india*
[15] *Tibetan Refugees' Rights and Services in India - Digital Commons @ DU*, *https://digitalcommons.du.edu/cgi/viewcontent.cgi?article=1631&context =hrhw*
[16] *Central Tibetan Relief Committee ,* *https://www.nextias.com/ca/current-affairs/11-04-2022/central-tibetan-relief-committee*
[17] *Chakma, Hajongs in Arunachal Pradesh Face 'Uncertain Future' as Government Plans Relocation - Land Conflict Watch,* *https://www.landconflictwatch.org/conflicts/Chakma-hajongs-in-arunachal-pradesh-face-uncertain-future-as-government-plans-relocation*

provides compelling evidence of this recognition [18]. The LARR Act is specifically designed to protect the rights of landowners, ensuring fair compensation and rehabilitation upon land acquisition [19]. This legislation would not typically be invoked for acquiring land from refugees living in temporary shelters without legal ownership. The fact that the government applied the LARR Act in this instance signifies an unequivocal acknowledgment of the Chakma as landowners with rights to compensation and resettlement, a status fundamentally inconsistent with that of temporary refugees.

The assertion that the Chakma and Hajongs live in refugee camps or structured settlement clusters is also directly contradicted by the reality on the ground. They reside in recognized villages, deeply integrated into the very fabric of Arunachal Pradesh. This is unlike the often more segregated and formally administered settlements established for other refugee groups, such as the Tibetan communities. Historical accounts confirm that the Chakma and Hajongs were settled in specific areas of NEFA with the agreement of local authorities and tribal leaders [20]. Having lived in the region for over six decades, the Chakma and Hajongs have developed significant social, religious, and economic ties to Arunachal Pradesh [21]. This established presence and integration into recognized villages, as opposed to confinement in temporary camps, further debunks the persistent myth surrounding their living situation.

---

[18]
https://www.indiacode.nic.in/bitstream/123456789/19895/1/the_right_to_fair_compensation_and_transparency_in_land_acquisition,_rehabilitation_and_resettlement_act,_2013..pdf
[19] *The Right to Fair Compensation and Transparency in Land Acquisition, Rehabilitation, and Resettlement Act, 2013 | O.P. Jindal Global University, https://jgu.edu.in/jsgp/jindal-policy-research-lab/the-right-to-fair-compensation-and-transparency-in-land-acquisition-rehabilitation-and-resettlement-act-2013/*
[20] *Chakma of Arunachal Pradesh – CRDO, https://crdo.chakma.in/Chakma-of-arunachal-pradesh/*
[21] *The Chakma-Hajong challenge - Observer Research Foundation, https://www.orfonline.org/expert-speak/chakma-hajong-challenge*

Land ownership is a powerful indicator of integration and citizenship. It provides a tangible stake in fostering economic independence through agriculture and contributing to social integration within established communities [22]. Despite possessing land rights and having resided in India for six decades, the Chakma and Hajongs in Arunachal Pradesh continue to be denied recognition as citizens, particularly by the state government. This is despite the fact that over 95% of them are by-birth citizens under Section 3(1)(a) of the Citizenship Act, 1955. As a result, they continue to struggle for "at par" rights alongside other citizens of the state [23].

The Supreme Court has repeatedly directed the government to process the citizenship applications of 4,637 Chakma and Hajongs—part of the original migrant group—who seek naturalization under the Citizenship Act, 1955. [24] However, a proposal for **"limited citizenship"** without land ownership rights or Scheduled Tribe status has met with resistance [25] from Chakma and Hajongs. The fact remains that the Chakma and Hajongs' land ownership, combined with their prolonged presence and legal entitlement as citizens, positions them as a community seeking formal recognition as integrated members of India, a status that transcends the temporary label of refugees awaiting repatriation.

---

[22] *land use pattern and food security of stateless: profile of arunachal Chakma,* *https://www.worldwidejournals.com/indian-journal-of-applied-research-(IJAR)/recent_issues_pdf/2019/October/land-use-pattern-and-food-security-of-stateless-profile-of-arunachal-Chakma_October_2019_1571897281_9711789.pdf*
[23] *Chakma of Arunachal Pradesh – CRDO,* *https://crdo.chakma.in/Chakma-of-arunachal-pradesh/*
[24] *Chakma, Hajongs in Arunachal Pradesh Face 'Uncertain Future' as Government Plans Relocation - Land Conflict Watch,* *https://www.landconflictwatch.org/conflicts/Chakma-hajongs-in-arunachal-pradesh-face-uncertain-future-as-government-plans-relocation*
[25] *The Chakma-Hajong challenge - Observer Research Foundation,* *https://www.orfonline.org/expert-speak/chakma-hajong-challenge*

The evidence presented in this chapter compellingly demonstrates that the Chakma and Hajongs of Arunachal Pradesh cannot be accurately characterized as refugees living in camps. Their history of land ownership, facilitated by the Indian government as part of a planned resettlement, their integration into recognized villages, and the state's acknowledgment of their property rights through the application of the LARR Act all point towards a settled community with established ties to the land. This situation stands in marked contrast to the typical experiences of refugees in India, including Tibetan refugees, who generally do not possess individual land ownership rights. The persistent narrative that casts the Chakma and Hajongs as refugees in camps overlooks their lived reality and their rights as long-term residents. It is imperative to re-evaluate the prevailing discourse and move beyond the loosely associated "refugee" label. The Chakma and Hajongs of Arunachal Pradesh are not transient sojourners but a community of landowners who have been integrated into the state for decades. Their land ownership should be a central consideration in any discussions regarding their legal status and their rightful place within the Indian nation. Recognizing their reality as integrated landowners is crucial for fostering a more accurate and just understanding of their position in Arunachal Pradesh.

1.2. RESIDENCE: RECOGNIZED VILLAGES VS. DESIGNATED REFUGEE CAMPS

One of the most striking differences between the Chakma & Hajongs and Tibetan refugees lies in their settlement patterns and administrative categorization. The Chakma and Hajongs in Arunachal Pradesh are not placed in isolated refugee camps but reside in recognized census villages that fall within the ambit of India's formal administrative framework. This crucial distinction not only undermines the refugee label but also demonstrates their integration into local governance structures. In contrast, Tibetan refugees are settled in designated refugee camps across India, such as those in Miao and Tezu in Arunachal Pradesh, Dharamshala in Himachal Pradesh, and Bylakuppe and Mundgod in Karnataka. These Tibetan settlements are administered separately under the jurisdiction of the Central Tibetan Administration (CTA) and are governed by a policy framework distinct from the local administration [26].

The legal and administrative implications of these differing settlement structures are profound. Chakma and Hajong villages are recognized as regular revenue villages under state and central government jurisdiction, with residents participating in local governance and being subject to the same taxation, land ownership regulations, and legal obligations as other Indian citizens. This reflects their integration into the Indian polity, a status fundamentally incompatible with the definition of "refugee." In contrast, Tibetan settlements operate with a degree of legal and political autonomy, with governance structures that reinforce their status as a community awaiting potential repatriation or a special political resolution. Tibetan refugee camps function with a clear acknowledgment of their impermanence, as their population remains classified as "foreigners" under the Foreigners Act, 1946, and their residence is governed by a temporary lease policy, renewable every 20 years.

The Chakma and Hajongs' residing in established villages not only signifies a pathway toward full integration but also challenges the refugee narrative imposed upon them. Unlike Tibetan refugees, who remain administratively distinct from the local population, Chakma and Hajongs function under the same bureaucratic and governance structures as other Indian residents. This difference is not merely a technicality; it speaks to the broader question of political and legal recognition. The continued

---

[26] *South Asia's Tibetan Refugee Community Is Shrinking, Imperiling Its Long-Term Future, https://www.migrationpolicy.org/article/tibetan-refugees-india*

classification of Chakma and Hajongs as "foreigners" in Arunachal Pradesh is an anachronism, given their decades-long presence in the region, land ownership rights, and by-birth citizenship under Indian law. Therefore, while Tibetan refugee camps reinforce a legally separate and politically distinct status, the Chakma and Hajongs' residence in formally recognized villages underscores their rightful claim to equal citizenship, not a temporary asylum.

1.3. DEPENDENCE: SELF RELIANCE VS. RELIANCE ON HUMANITARIAN AGENCIES

A fundamental characteristic of refugee populations is their reliance on international humanitarian aid, a feature that sharply differentiates Tibetan refugees from the Chakma and Hajongs. The Chakma and Hajongs in Arunachal Pradesh have never been dependent on international organizations such as the United Nations High Commissioner for Refugees (UNHCR) or other global humanitarian agencies for their sustenance. Their survival and economic integration have been solely driven by self-reliance, local economic participation, and engagement with India's formal governance structures. In contrast, Tibetan refugees receive significant financial and material assistance from international humanitarian agencies, reinforcing their continued recognition as a distinct refugee population.

This dependency on international aid among Tibetan refugees is a direct consequence of their recognized refugee status under global conventions. Even though India is not a signatory to the 1951 Refugee Convention or its 1967 Protocol, the Tibetan refugee community has been treated as a unique case due to historical and geopolitical considerations. The Central Tibetan Administration (CTA), functioning as a government-in-exile, coordinates substantial funding from international donors, including foreign governments, NGOs, and international refugee welfare programs. This aid covers essential services such as education, healthcare, and community development within designated Tibetan settlements. The structural reliance on external assistance distinguishes Tibetan refugees as a community that remains separate from the Indian socio-economic fabric, reinforcing their position as a non-integrated population awaiting a long-term political resolution.

In stark contrast, the Chakma and Hajongs' economic survival and community development have been achieved without external financial intervention. Their livelihoods are sustained through agriculture, trade, and other forms of economic participation within the Indian economy. This distinction is crucial because it dismantles the assumption that Chakma and Hajongs fit the conventional refugee framework, which presupposes financial and institutional dependence on international aid agencies. The very fact that Chakma and Hajongs are not beneficiaries of any UNHCR-administered refugee relief programs or foreign government assistance negates their classification as refugees in a traditional sense. Their status aligns more closely with that of other marginalized indigenous or displaced communities within India rather than that of a stateless refugee population dependent on foreign assistance.

Furthermore, the self-sustaining nature of the Chakma and Hajong communities speaks to their historical integration within the Indian polity. Unlike Tibetan refugees, who are subject to temporary land leases that reinforce their non-citizen status, Chakma and Hajongs were allotted land as part of a government rehabilitation program, enabling them to establish permanent livelihoods. This critical difference in settlement policy is a direct reflection of how the Chakma and Hajongs were never meant to be treated as refugees in perpetuity. Had they been intended to remain under international humanitarian oversight, as is the case with Tibetan refugees, they would have been placed under UNHCR protection and continued to receive external assistance. Instead, their economic self-sufficiency and integration into local markets and governance structures stand as strong evidence that their classification as refugees is both legally and practically inaccurate.

Thus, the absence of international humanitarian support for the Chakma and Hajongs is not merely an administrative oversight but a fundamental marker of their non-refugee status. Their self-reliance directly contradicts the defining characteristics of a refugee population, which typically requires sustained international aid due to displacement-induced economic vulnerability. By contrast, the Chakma and Hajongs' ability to sustain themselves without such aid underscores their rightful claim to full political and legal recognition within India. Their struggle is not one of refugee protection but of achieving equal rights as a historically settled and integrated community.

1.4. SEPARATE REHABILITATION POLICY: ABSENCE FOR CHAKMA-HAJONGS VS. EXISTENCE FOR TIBETAN REFUGEES

The existence of a separate rehabilitation policy is a fundamental indicator of the Indian government's perception of a community's legal and social status. A clearly defined policy framework for refugee rehabilitation reflects an explicit governmental acknowledgment of a group's statelessness or foreign origin. In this regard, a striking distinction emerges between the Chakma-Hajongs and Tibetan refugees: while Tibetan refugees benefit from a dedicated **Tibetan Rehabilitation Policy (TRP) 2014** [27], no equivalent framework exists for the Chakma and Hajongs in Arunachal Pradesh or elsewhere in India. This crucial difference underscores the argument that Chakma and Hajongs are not treated as refugees in the conventional sense.

---

[27] *Freedom Fighters & Rehabilitation Division,*
https://www.mha.gov.in/en/divisionofmha/freedom-fighters-rehabilitation-division

The Chakma and Hajongs were resettled in the 1960s under a centrally sponsored scheme that aimed to provide them with land and basic resources for self-sufficiency. However, this was not structured as a refugee rehabilitation program under international or national refugee policy frameworks. Instead, their resettlement mirrored other government-sponsored internal relocation initiatives for displaced communities, such as those undertaken for partition refugees or people displaced by dam projects. Unlike Tibetan refugees, the Chakma and Hajongs were not placed under the jurisdiction of any refugee relief agencies, nor were they granted the temporary asylum status typically associated with displaced foreign nationals.

In contrast, Tibetan refugees are governed by the **Tibetan Rehabilitation Policy, 2014**, formulated by the Ministry of Home Affairs (MHA) [28]. This policy provides a uniform framework for facilities and assistance across Indian states, recognizing the Tibetans' distinct status as an exiled community awaiting a long-term political resolution. The TRP 2014 grants Tibetans special provisions such as land lease extensions, government support for education, skill development, and reserved economic opportunities within their settlements. The policy is a formal acknowledgment that Tibetans are a stateless refugee population, requiring ongoing government intervention and support.

The absence of such a dedicated rehabilitation policy for the Chakma and Hajongs is not an oversight but a strong indication that the Indian state does not perceive them as a foreign refugee population in need of prolonged governmental oversight. Instead, their resettlement was intended as a permanent integration process rather than a temporary arrangement requiring continual external support. This is evident from the fact that Chakma and Hajongs were given **land allotments recorded in official land records**

---

[28] *The Tibetan Rehabilitation Policy, 2014. - Ministry of Home Affairs, https://www.mha.gov.in/sites/default/files/2022-08/FFR_ANNEXURE_A_17092019%5B1%5D.pdf*

(Chitta records), a legal measure signalling permanent settlement rather than transient refugee status. In contrast, Tibetan refugees are granted only renewable land leases, reinforcing their status as non-citizens with temporary residency rights.

Furthermore, the Chakma and Hajongs' demand for full citizenship rights and equal treatment within Arunachal Pradesh aligns with their historical status as residents seeking legal recognition, rather than as a distinct group requiring long-term rehabilitation. The repeated directives of the **Supreme Court of India** instructing the government to process Chakma and Hajong citizenship applications further demonstrate that their status is not that of a foreign refugee population but rather that of a settled community with rightful claims to full legal integration.

The absence of a separate rehabilitation policy for the Chakma and Hajongs, therefore, is not merely a technical administrative gap—it is a reflection of a fundamental legal and political distinction. While Tibetan refugees are categorized as a foreign refugee community requiring sustained government and international support, the Chakma and Hajongs are positioned within the framework of local governance and national integration. Any attempt to classify them as refugees ignores the historical and legal realities of their settlement and the Indian government's implicit acknowledgment of their permanent presence.

Thus, the presence of a structured rehabilitation policy for Tibetan refugees and its absence for the Chakma and Hajongs is a critical piece of evidence dismantling the misconception that Chakma and Hajongs are refugees. Their struggle is not for rehabilitation as displaced foreigners but for recognition as fully integrated members of Indian society, with rights and entitlements equal to those of any other citizen.

1.5. GOVERNANCE: CHAKMA-HAJONGS UNDER LOCAL ADMINISTRATION VS. TIBETAN REFUGEES UNDER SEPARATE EXILE GOVERNANCE

The administrative governance structures governing the Chakma and Hajongs of Arunachal Pradesh and other refugee communities in India, such as the Tibetans, present a stark contrast. The Chakma are governed by the local Indian administration, and they are subject to Indian laws and governance structures in the same way as any other citizens, unlike the Tibetans, who are administered through a parallel administrative structure coordinated by an exile government.

This crucial distinction underscores the argument that Chakma and Hajongs in Arunachal Pradesh do not fit the conventional definition of refugees as recognized in international or Indian legal frameworks.

(a) *Governance of Chakma in Arunachal Pradesh:* The Chakma and Hajongs residing in Arunachal Pradesh are administratively governed by the state government and local governance bodies under the Indian legal framework. Their interactions with the government occur through mainstream governance structures such as the Deputy Commissioner, local administration, and other local administration mechanisms. Unlike recognized refugees who receive special administrative oversight from dedicated agencies such as the United Nations High Commissioner for Refugees (UNHCR) or the Indian government's specific refugee-oriented bodies, the Chakma in Arunachal Pradesh are fully embedded within India's legal and administrative machinery.

Moreover, 95% of Chakma and Hajongs in Arunachal Pradesh are citizens by birth under Section 3(1)(a) of the Citizenship Act, 1955, while the rest are eligible for citizenship under Section 5(1)(a) as per the Supreme Court's directives. This stands in contrast to refugees who typically lack citizenship status in their host countries.

Their inclusion in India's electoral process and governance structures further cements their status as integral members of Indian society rather than displaced refugees in need of a distinct administrative mechanism.

(b) *Governance of Tibetan Refugees: A Separate Administrative Framework*

The Tibetan refugees in India operate under an entirely different administrative model. The Government of India, through the Ministry of Home Affairs' Freedom Fighters & Rehabilitation (FFR) [29] wing, coordinates with the Central Tibetan Administration (CTA), often referred to as the Tibetan Government-in-Exile. This administrative setup provides a unique governance mechanism that functions outside the conventional state administration governing Indian citizens.

The CTA operates through the Central Tibetan Relief Committee (CTRC), which oversees Tibetan settlements and manages welfare, education, and governance within the Tibetan refugee community. Additionally, Tibetan refugees have their own local governance structures within settlements, working in tandem with the exile government. This distinct administrative model highlights their status as a community in political exile, which is fundamentally different from the Chakma and Hajongs in Arunachal Pradesh, who are subject solely to Indian governance without any parallel administrative oversight.

(c) *Legal and Political Identity of the Chakma & Hajongs: Why They Are Not Refugees:* In international refugee law, as outlined by the 1951 Refugee Convention and its 1967 Protocol, refugees are typically defined as individuals who have fled persecution and require protection in a host country where they do not possess rights equivalent to citizens. In the case of Tibetans in

---

[29] *https://www.mha.gov.in/en/divisionofmha/freedom-fighters-rehabilitation-division*

India, their governance structure aligns with this definition, as they are governed by their own exile administration rather than the full apparatus of Indian governance.

By contrast, the Chakma and Hajongs in Arunachal Pradesh, despite being displaced from their ancestral lands due to events such as the construction of the Kaptai Dam and religious violence in erstwhile East Pakistan (now Bangladesh), were resettled by the Indian government with the explicit intention of integration. Unlike Tibetans, the Chakma and Hajongs were not placed in settlements with separate governance structures but were instead given land and placed under the same administrative system as Indian citizens. Their assimilation into local governance structures, coupled with their electoral participation and access to state and central government benefits, negates their classification as refugees in the conventional sense.

Chakma and Hajongs as a Rehabilitated and Integrated Community: The governance structures overseeing the Chakma and Hajong communities in Arunachal Pradesh provide a strong administrative argument against their characterization as refugees. The Chakma and Hajongs are fully integrated into India's local governance system, participate in political and social processes, and are recognized within the Indian legal framework as rightful residents and citizens. In contrast, Tibetan refugees function under a dual administrative system that maintains their identity as a distinct community in exile.

Thus, while the Chakma and Hajongs of Arunachal Pradesh may have been displaced historically, their administrative governance, legal recognition, and integration into Indian society substantiate the argument that they are not refugees in the conventional sense but rather a rehabilitated community that has become an inseparable part of India's sociopolitical fabric

1.6. POPULATION CENSUS: INCLUSION IN NATIONAL CENSUS VS. SEPARATE CENSUS

The General Population Census of India, conducted every ten years, is far more than a routine tally of heads. It is a monumental undertaking—a cornerstone of governance that maps the nation's demographic, social, and cultural contours. This census does not merely count; it defines. It informs policy-making, drives resource allocation, and underpins the National Population Register (NPR), shaping the very framework of India's future. To be included in this census is to be recognized as a thread in the nation's fabric, a permanent resident woven into its enduring identity. To be excluded is to remain on the margins, a transient figure awaiting an uncertain fate. This brings us to a critical distinction: the Chakma and Hajongs of Arunachal Pradesh are counted in this decadal census, while Tibetan refugees are not. This is no minor detail—it is a profound marker of belonging that shatters the conventional refugee label so often misapplied to the Chakma and Hajongs.

The Census: A Reflection of Permanence

India's decadal census is a mirror held up to the nation, reflecting those who belong within its borders—not as guests, but as rooted inhabitants. It captures the lives of citizens and long-term residents, providing the data that fuels infrastructure, education, healthcare, and electoral representation. For the state, it is a declaration of who constitutes the "general population [30]"—those with a stake in India's present and a claim to its tomorrow. Refugees, by contrast, are typically absent from this mirror. Their status as temporary sojourners—often tethered to international oversight or special administrative policies—demands separate enumeration. This

---

[30] *Office of the Registrar General & Census Commissioner, Ministry of Home Affairs, Government of India, https://new.census.gov.in/*

exclusion is not a mere technicality; it is a deliberate signal of impermanence, a reminder that their presence is conditional, their future elsewhere.

The Tibetan refugees in India embody this separation. Under the Tibetan Rehabilitation Policy of 2014, the Central Tibetan Administration (CTA) conducts a distinct census every five years, counting those scattered across settlements and beyond. This parallel process, monitored but not integrated by the Indian government, underscores their status as foreigners—refugees in waiting, not residents in staying. Their exclusion from the national census is a quiet but firm acknowledgment of their temporariness, a boundary drawn between them and the broader Indian populace.

The Chakma and Hajongs: Counted, Claimed, and Rooted

Now consider the Chakma and Hajongs. Since their resettlement in Arunachal Pradesh in the 1960s, following their displacement from the Chittagong Hill Tracts, they have been enumerated in India's decadal census alongside their neighbours—farmers, teachers, shopkeepers, and families who call this land home. This inclusion is not a bureaucratic oversight or a statistical quirk; it is a deliberate act of recognition. To be counted in the census is to be seen by the state—not as a shadow passing through, but as a community with roots, a population with permanence. For the Chakma and Hajongs, this is more than a number on a page; it is a validation of their existence, a lifeline tethering them to the soil they have tilled for generations.

Imagine the weight of this moment for a Chakma and Hajong elder, standing before a census enumerator, his name and family recorded not as outsiders, but as part of India's story. "They count us," he might say, his voice steady with pride, "because we are here to stay. This is our home, not a camp." This is not just data collection—it is an emotional anchor, a rebuttal to decades of whispers branding them as interlopers. The census binds them to the nation's narrative, affirming that they are not a people apart, but a people integral to India's demographic landscape.

Why this Distinction Cuts Deep

The inclusion of the Chakma and Hajongs in the decadal census is a powerful lens through which to dismantle the "refugee" myth that clings to them like a stubborn shadow. Let's break it down:

- **Recognition of Permanent Residency**: The census is a roll call of India's enduring population. By including the Chakma and Hajongs, the state acknowledges their right to remain—not as refugees on borrowed time, but as residents with a future etched in Arunachal's hills. This is a tacit endorsement of their permanence, a stamp of legitimacy that no political rhetoric can erase.

- **Rejection of the "Temporary" Narrative**: Refugees, by definition, are transient—wayfarers awaiting return or relocation. Their exclusion from national censuses reflects this fleeting status. The Chakma and Hajongs, however, are not sidelined in this way. Their presence in the census declares them free of that impermanence, their lives intertwined with India's trajectory rather than dangling in limbo.

- **Affirmation of National Identity**: To be counted is to belong. The census weaves the Chakma and Hajongs into the tapestry of India's broader community, granting them a place not as foreigners or wards of charity, but as contributors to the nation's shared identity. It is a quiet yet unyielding assertion of their Indianness.

This is not about dry statistics; it is about dignity, about truth. The "refugee" label, when flung at the Chakma and Hajongs, ignores the state's own evidence—their legal migration, their planned rehabilitation, their decades of integration. The census stands as a bulwark against this misinformation, a record that speaks louder than divisive slogans or outdated prejudices.

A Stark Contrast: Chakma & Hajongs and Tibetans Side by Side

To sharpen this point, let's place the Chakma and Hajongs beside the Tibetan refugees once more. The Tibetans' separate census, orchestrated by the CTA, is a constant echo of their outsider status. It marks them as a population apart, their lives tracked not for integration, but for management—temporary guests under India's hospitality, not permanent kin within its fold. The Chakma and Hajongs face no such segregation. Their names, their households, their futures are recorded alongside all others in the national census, their data fueling the same plans that shape India's growth. This is not a subtle difference; it is a chasm, a testament to the Chakma and Hajongs' rootedness where the Tibetans remain unmoored.

The Final Word: A Census of Clarity

The inclusion of the Chakma and Hajongs in India's decadal census is not just a fact—it is a foundation. It is a vital piece of evidence that topples the flimsy "refugee" narrative and plants a flag of truth in its place. To call them refugees is to defy the state's own ledger; to dismiss the emotional and historical ties they have forged over half a century, and to perpetuate a lie that serves only to wound. The Chakma and Hajongs are not waiting for a boat to carry them away; they are building lives on land they have made their own. Their place in the census is their victory—a quiet, unshakable proof of belonging.

Let this be the closing note: the Chakma and Hajongs are not refugees, not by any measure that holds weight. They are counted because they count—because India, in its own meticulous records, has claimed them as its own. To honour this truth is to honour their struggle, their resilience, and their rightful home in Arunachal Pradesh.

1.7. THE FOREIGNERS ACT OF 1946: THE LEGAL BEDROCK OF REFUGEE STATUS

The Chakma and Hajongs of Arunachal Pradesh are frequently mischaracterized as refugees, a label that crumbles under scrutiny when their legal status is examined. At the heart of this misclassification lies a striking anomaly: unlike Tibetan refugees and other refugee groups in India, the Chakma and Hajongs are not subject to the Foreigners Act of 1946—a law that defines and governs the presence of foreigners and refugees alike. This exemption is not a trivial footnote but a deliberate, historically rooted policy that sets the Chakma and Hajongs apart, challenging the very definition, characteristics, and traits of a conventional refugee. Through a critical analysis of this legal distinction, juxtaposed against the treatment of Tibetan refugees, it becomes evident that the Chakma and Hajongs' status in India is not one of temporary asylum but of intended permanence—a reality that carries profound emotional and legal weight.

A Legal Distinction That Defies the Refugee Label

To unravel why the Chakma and Hajongs' exemption is so consequential, we must first understand the Foreigners Act of 1946. Enacted in the twilight of British rule, this law remains India's primary mechanism for regulating foreign nationals. It empowers the government to monitor, restrict, and, if necessary, deport individuals who are not Indian citizens, defining their entry, stay, and departure with precision. In the absence of a dedicated refugee law in India, refugees—those fleeing persecution or disaster across borders—are typically subsumed under this Act. Their status as foreigners subjects them to stringent oversight: registration requirements, periodic renewals of stay permits, and the ever-present spectre of deportation. For groups like Tibetans, Afghans, or Sri Lankan Tamils, the Act is the legal tether that binds them to a transient existence, marking them as outsiders granted sanctuary but not belonging.

The conventional refugee, by definition, occupies this precarious space. They are not citizens; they are not permanent residents. Their presence is conditional, often dictated by geopolitical circumstances or humanitarian goodwill, and their rights are curtailed by the framework of the Foreigners Act. This legal classification is more than a bureaucratic detail—it is a reflection of their impermanence, a constant reminder that their home lies elsewhere, beyond India's borders.

The Chakma and Hajongs' Exemption: A Policy of Protection, Not Oversight

Yet, the Chakma and Hajongs stand apart from this paradigm. They are not tracked, regulated, or restrained by the Foreigners Act of 1946—a fact that shatters the refugee narrative applied to them. This is not a lapse in governance or an administrative quirk; it is a purposeful decision etched into India's historical and legal fabric. A key piece of evidence is the Government of India's Letter No. 21/48/62-F. IV(B), issued on January 3, 1964. Addressed to all state governments, this directive explicitly addressed the treatment of minority communities displaced from East Pakistan (now Bangladesh), including the Chakma and Hajongs. It mandated that these individuals—fleeing persecution, communal violence, or, in the Chakma' case, the devastating loss of their lands to the Kaptai Dam—were not to be prosecuted under the Passport (Entry into

India) Act of 1920 or the Foreigners Act of 1946 without prior consent from the central government [31].

This was no blanket amnesty for all migrants but a targeted shield for persecuted minorities, a recognition of their unique plight. For the Chakma and Hajongs, displaced in the early 1960s and resettled in Arunachal Pradesh, this directive translated into a legal sanctuary. They were not to be treated as foreigners or refugees under the law's watchful eye. Instead, the government carved out an exception, signalling that their presence was not temporary, their status not contingent. They were allocated land, included in national records, and spared the legal shackles that define refugee life. This exemption, far from incidental, was a cornerstone of a broader policy to integrate rather than merely shelter—a promise of permanence etched in bureaucratic ink.

Tibetan Refugees: A Study in Contrast

The Tibetan refugees, arriving in India from 1959 onward after the Chinese occupation of Tibet, offer a stark counterpoint. Classified unequivocally as foreigners under the Foreigners Act, their lives are governed by its provisions. They carry Registration Certificates (RCs), renewable documents that tether their residency to bureaucratic approval. Their movements are restricted, their rights limited, and their status perpetually temporary. Housed in settlements like Dharamshala, they exist in a liminal space—grateful for refuge, yet marked as outsiders by the law. The Act looms over them, a constant reminder of their foreignness, their dependence on India's goodwill rather than a claim to its soil.

---

[31] *MHA guidelines to State Governments regarding treatment of Minorities from East Pakistan, Letter No. 21/48/62-F. IV(B), File No. 13024/5/73-AP-II, Development and regulatory measures, Security matters - Settlement of Chakma Refugees in Arunachal Pradesh (National Archives of India)*

Compare this to the Chakma and Hajongs: no RCs, no renewals, no legal designation as foreigners. Where Tibetans are managed as a distinct, transient population, the Chakma and Hajongs were resettled with intent—given land, woven into the fabric of Arunachal Pradesh, and freed from the Foreigners Act's constraints. This contrast is not subtle; it is a chasm. If the Chakma and Hajongs were refugees in the conventional sense, why do they not bear the same legal burdens as their Tibetan counterparts? Why does the Foreigners Act, the litmus test of refugee status in India, pass them by?

If Chakma and Hajongs Were Refugees, Why the Exemption?

This question strikes at the core of the debate. The legal definition of a refugee—someone fleeing across borders, seeking asylum, and governed as a foreigner—demands a framework like the Foreigners Act. If the Chakma and Hajongs were truly refugees, their presence in Arunachal Pradesh would fall under its purview, their lives regulated as those of Tibetans or Sri Lankan Tamils. Yet, they are untouched by it. This absence is not a loophole but a loud declaration: the Indian state does not view them as refugees. To subject them to the Act would be to treat them as foreigners, a status the government has consistently rejected since 1964.

The 1964 letter was not a one-off gesture but part of a sustained approach. For decades, the Chakma and Hajongs have lived without the legal precarity that defines refugee existence—no deportations, no permit renewals, no segregation into camps. Their exemption has endured, a testament to an unspoken covenant: they were not meant to be temporary guests but a people with roots in India. As one Chakma elder might say, voice trembling with the weight of memory, "We did not come to beg for shelter. We were given a home, and the law knows it." This is not the language of refugees; it is the cry of belonging, backed by a legal reality that refuses to confine them to the margins.

Emotional Weight and Historical Depth

The Chakma' story is not just a legal argument—it is a human saga. Uprooted by the Kaptai Dam, their homeland submerged under water, they crossed borders not as invaders or transients but as survivors seeking a new beginning. India's response was not cold bureaucracy but a hand extended in solidarity. The 1964 directive was a lifeline, a shield against the alienation of refugee status. While Tibetans remain caught in a legal limbo, their future uncertain, the Chakma and Hajongs were offered stability—land to till, a place to call their own. This was not asylum; it was adoption, a quiet but resolute act of inclusion.

The emotional resonance of this distinction cannot be overstated. For the Chakma and Hajongs, exemption from the Foreigners Act is more than a legal technicality—it is a validation of their identity, a bulwark against the erasure of their history. It whispers to every child born in Arunachal Pradesh, every elder who remembers the migration: *You are not strangers here. You belong.* Contrast this with the Tibetan experience—grateful yet rootless, tethered to a law that marks them as perpetual outsiders and foreigners. The Chakma and Hajongs' exemption is their anchor, their proof of permanence in a world that too often casts the displaced adrift.

The Final Word

The Chakma and Hajongs are not refugees—not by law, not by history, not by the land they have made their own. The Foreigners Act of 1946, the legal hallmark of refugee status in India, has never claimed them. This is no accident but a deliberate choice, a policy born in 1964 and upheld across generations, distinguishing them from Tibetans and others bound by the Act's chains. To call them refugees is to ignore the evidence, to erase the intent behind their exemption—a intent not of temporary refuge but of enduring belonging.

Let the record stand clear: the Chakma and Hajongs' roots run deep in Arunachal Pradesh, unburdened by the legal shadows that define conventional refugees. They are not a people in waiting, poised to return to a lost homeland. They are home, their place affirmed by a nation that chose to embrace rather than merely shelter them. The Foreigners Act, with its cold grip on outsiders, stops at their doorstep—a silent, unshakable testament to their truth. In the end, the Chakma and Hajongs are not refugees; they are India's own, their story a defiant rebuttal to any label that dares suggest otherwise. Here they stand, exempt and enduring, a living legacy of a promise kept.

1.8. VOTING RIGHTS: WHY CHAKMA-HAJONGS ARE NOT REFUGEES

One of the most definitive markers of citizenship in any nation is the right to vote—a right that separates full members of a polity from temporary residents or foreign nationals. As of 2024, approximately 9,300 Chakma and Hajongs are enrolled in Arunachal's electoral rolls and actively participate in both Assembly and Parliamentary elections. In contrast, Tibetan and other refugee groups in India are denied this right, as they are legally classified as foreigners or refugees. This stark difference is not merely administrative but has profound legal, political, and social implications.

Understanding the Constitutional Foundation of Voting Rights

In India, voting rights in Assembly and Parliamentary elections are exclusively reserved for Indian citizens, as enshrined in Article

326 of the Constitution. This article guarantees universal adult suffrage to all citizens aged 18 and above, reinforcing the inalienable link between electoral participation and citizenship [32].

Refugees, as a category of individuals who have sought asylum due to persecution in their country of origin, do not automatically qualify for citizenship and, consequently, do not enjoy voting rights. The Indian government's stance has been consistent in this regard—foreign nationals, including Tibetan refugees who have lived in India for decades, remain disenfranchised unless they take legal steps to acquire Indian citizenship under applicable laws.

The Case for Chakma and Hajong Citizenship

The fact that Chakma and Hajongs have been granted voting rights strongly indicates that they do not fit within the conventional definition of refugees. In democracies worldwide, the right to vote is a sovereign privilege, typically granted only to citizens or those on a defined pathway to citizenship. Given that Chakma and Hajongs have been included in the electoral rolls, their legal status aligns more closely with Indian citizens rather than stateless or transient refugee populations.

Additionally, if Chakma and Hajongs were truly refugees, they would have been subject to the same political restrictions as Tibetan refugees, Rohingyas, or other displaced groups within India. The legal system does not selectively grant voting rights to refugees while denying the same to others. The inclusion of Chakma and Hajongs in the electoral process is thus a clear acknowledgment of their legal and civic integration within India, distinguishing them from recognized refugee groups.

Contrasting the Status of Tibetan Refugees

---

[32] *Election Commission of India, Can a non-citizen of India become a voter in the electoral rolls in India? https://voters.eci.gov.in/HomePageFaq*

Tibetan refugees, despite being well-settled in India since 1959, do not enjoy voting rights. Their community exists under a unique political arrangement wherein they are governed by the Central Tibetan Administration (CTA), a government-in-exile based in Dharamshala. India recognizes their special status but does not extend citizenship or electoral participation to them en-masse. Even Tibetan refugees born in India have to apply for citizenship separately and face procedural hurdles.

This difference in treatment further highlights the fundamental distinction between the Chakma & Hajongs and Tibetan refugees. If the Chakma and Hajongs were genuinely considered refugees, they would have faced similar exclusions. Instead, they have been accorded rights that place them on the same footing as other Indian citizens.

The Legal and Political Implications

The granting of voting rights to Chakma and Hajongs is not a minor administrative decision; it is a legal and political acknowledgment of their status within the Indian Union. Refugee status is inherently temporary, while citizenship is permanent. By allowing Chakma and Hajongs to participate in democratic processes, the Indian state has recognized their legal belonging, making the refugee label inapplicable to their case.

Moreover, the continued labelling of Chakma and Hajongs as refugees despite their electoral participation is a misrepresentation that denies them their rightful place in Indian society. It perpetuates a false narrative that undermines their historical and legal claims to Indian citizenship.

Conclusion: Breaking the Refugee Stereotype

The evidence overwhelmingly supports the assertion that Chakma and Hajongs do not fit the traditional definition of refugees.

Unlike Tibetan refugees, who remain politically disenfranchised, Chakma and Hajongs have been granted one of the most fundamental rights of citizenship: the right to vote. This distinction is not incidental; it is the result of legal recognition that acknowledges their integration into Indian society.

Continuing to refer to Chakma and Hajongs as refugees is not just inaccurate—it is a distortion of reality that marginalizes a community that has already met the legal and civic criteria for Indian citizenship. If voting rights define political belonging, then Chakma and Hajongs, by all standards, belong unequivocally to India.

1.9. IDENTITY DOCUMENTS AS MARKERS OF BELONGING

Identity documents are fundamental to establishing one's legal status in a country. They serve not only as proof of identity but also as indicators of an individual's civic rights, including employment opportunities, mobility, and political participation. The type of documents one holds can significantly determine whether they are recognized as a citizen, a foreigner, or a refugee. When comparing the Chakma & Hajongs and Tibetan refugees in India, a stark difference emerges in the nature and implications of their identity documents.

Chakma and Hajongs: Holders of Indian Identity Documents

Chakma and Hajongs possess key Indian identity documents, including Indian Passport, Voter ID (EPIC), Aadhaar Card, PAN Card, and Driving License. These documents are issued by government agencies and are widely accepted as proof of residence, taxation compliance, and, in the case of Voter ID, electoral participation [33]. The issuance of these documents underscores Chakma and Hajongs' legal presence within India and their integration into Indian systems. The presence of Chakma and Hajongs in voter rolls further solidifies their claim to citizenship since voting rights in Parliamentary and Assembly elections are constitutionally reserved for Indian citizens under Article 326.

A significant number of Chakma and Hajongs, particularly those who have voting rights, are legally recognized as Indian citizens. The fact that they are granted identity documents indistinguishable from those of other Indian citizens demonstrates their formal acceptance into India's legal and administrative framework. If Chakma and Hajongs were indeed refugees, they would not possess documents that affirm their citizenship and civic participation.

Tibetan Refugees: The Registration Certificate (RC) – A Temporary Status [34]

In contrast, Tibetan refugees do not possess Indian identity documents such as Voter ID or Aadhaar in the same manner as Indian citizens. Instead, they are issued Registration Certificates (RCs), which serve as their primary identity document in India. These RCs are not proof of Indian citizenship but rather a mechanism for the Indian government to track and regulate their presence. Tibetan refugees must renew their RCs every five years, reinforcing their status as non-citizens under government oversight. The very existence of this renewal process indicates the temporary nature of their stay and the fact that they remain foreign nationals despite decades of residence in India.

---

[33] *Livelaw.in, which Documents Prove Indian Citizenship?,* *https://www.livelaw.in/columns/which-documents-prove-indian-citizenship-153027*
[34] *Tibetan Legal Association, Registration Certificate , https://tibetanlegalassociation.org/en/legal-overview-of-the-status-of-tibetans-in-india/*

The inability of Tibetan refugees to obtain citizenship-related documents en masse, despite their long-standing presence in India, clearly separates their status from that of Chakma and Hajongs. While Chakma and Hajongs possess documents that affirm their citizenship, Tibetan refugees remain in a bureaucratic limbo, dependent on government policies for their continued stay.

The Legal and Administrative Significance of Identity Documents

In India, no single document serves as absolute proof of citizenship. However, certain documents are widely accepted as indicators of citizenship:

- **Indian Passport** – Issued exclusively to Indian citizens by the Government of India, making it one of the strongest proofs of nationality.

- **Voter ID (EPIC Card)** – While not an automatic proof of citizenship, it is issued only to Indian citizens who are eligible to vote in national and state elections.

- **Aadhaar Card** – Used for identification and welfare schemes but not legally recognized as proof of citizenship.

- **Birth Certificate** – If issued under the Registration of Births and Deaths Act, 1969, it helps establish citizenship by birth in accordance with the Citizenship Act.

The absence of these documents in the case of Tibetan refugees—and their widespread possession by Chakma and Hajongs—further highlights the fundamental distinction between the two groups. The presence of Chakma and Hajongs in India's electoral system and their possession of officially recognized documents fundamentally contradicts their classification as refugees.

Why Identity Documents Matter

The possession of Indian identity documents by Chakma and Hajongs is not just a bureaucratic detail—it is a strong legal and administrative assertion of their status in India. If Chakma and Hajongs were indeed refugees, they would not have access to Voter ID or other citizenship-linked documents, just as Tibetan refugees do not. The difference in documentation reflects a deeper truth: Chakma and Hajongs have been absorbed into the Indian legal framework, while Tibetan refugees remain legally separate from Indian citizens.

Moreover, the continued classification of Chakma and Hajongs as refugees despite their possession of Indian identity documents is an erroneous portrayal that undermines their legitimate status. The very institutions responsible for issuing these documents recognize Chakma and Hajongs as part of the Indian citizenry, making any attempt to label them as refugees not just misleading but legally and administratively incorrect.

Conclusion: Identity as a Reflection of Citizenship

Identity documents are not mere papers; they define one's legal status, rights, and place within a nation. Chakma and Hajongs, with their voter IDs, Passports, Aadhaar, PAN, and driving licenses, have been fully integrated into India's administrative and electoral systems—rights that refugees are not granted. Tibetan refugees, on the other hand, remain legally distinct from Indian citizens, relying on temporary registration certificates that reaffirm their foreign status.

Continuing to categorize Chakma and Hajongs as refugees is an outdated and misleading assertion that does not align with their legal standing. If identity documents are the key indicators of citizenship and legal belonging, then Chakma and Hajongs, by all rational and legal measures, are not refugees. Their place in India is not one of transient asylum-seekers but of rightful members of the Indian nation.

1.10. REFUGEE STATUS DETERMINATION: LEGAL RECOGNITION AND INTERNATIONAL STANDARDS

Refugee Status Determination (RSD)[35] is a critical process that establishes whether an individual qualifies as a refugee under international law. This process is managed by the United Nations High Commissioner for Refugees (UNHCR) and is vital for providing asylum seekers with legal protection and assistance. The distinction between those who undergo this process and those who do not is a key indicator of their status. A comparative analysis of the Chakma & Hajongs and Tibetan refugees within this framework highlights a crucial difference—one that underscores why Chakma and Hajongs do not fit the conventional definition of refugees.

Chakma and Hajongs: Not Recognized as Refugees by UNHCR

The Chakma and Hajongs are not recognized as refugees by UNHCR and are not covered under the UNHCR's Refugee Status Determination (RSD) process. This is a decisive factor in proving that the Chakma do not belong to the legally defined category of refugees. Unlike stateless or asylum-seeking populations, Chakma and Hajongs have not been subject to international refugee protocols, nor have they been processed through the UNHCR's mechanisms for refugee assistance.

Furthermore, the Chakma and Hajongs in Arunachal Pradesh have integrated into the Indian legal framework, with many holding

---

[35] *UNHCR, Refugee Status Determination,*
https://help.unhcr.org/india/refugee-status-determination-2/

Indian identity documents such as Voter ID, Passport, Aadhaar, and PAN cards. These documents signify their legal acceptance within India, reinforcing that their presence is neither temporary nor subject to refugee policies. Had they been refugees, they would have been under UNHCR jurisdiction and dependent on asylum procedures rather than possessing Indian identity documents and participating in electoral processes.

Tibetan Refugees: A Different Category Under RSD

In contrast, Tibetan refugees have historically been treated as a distinct group by the Indian government. While they are not under the UNHCR's direct purview, their status is still managed under a special refugee policy. Tibetan refugees do not possess Indian identity documents like Chakma and Hajongs but instead hold Registration Certificates (RCs), which they must renew every five years. This requirement ensures that their presence is continuously monitored, reinforcing their status as non-citizens.

Although not governed by UNHCR in India, Tibetan refugees are recognized globally as a refugee population and have access to international advocacy under the broader framework of refugee protection. Unlike Chakma and Hajongs, whose status has evolved towards citizenship and legal integration, Tibetans remain in a transient category, aligning more closely with international refugee definitions.

UNHCR's RSD Process in India: Who Qualifies as a Refugee?

The UNHCR's Refugee Status Determination (RSD) in India primarily applies to asylum seekers and refugee groups not officially recognized by the Indian government. These include:

- **Afghan Refugees** – Many Afghan nationals, including ethnic Hindus and Sikhs, have sought asylum in India, with some receiving UNHCR refugee status.

- **Rohingya Refugees** – Stateless Rohingyas from Myanmar are registered with UNHCR, though India does not officially recognize them as refugees.

- **Somali and Sudanese Refugees** – Individuals fleeing conflict from these nations have also sought asylum through UNHCR in India.

- **Refugees from Other African and Middle Eastern Countries** – Small groups from Syria, Iraq, and other war-torn regions also fall under UNHCR protection.

A Distinction with Legal and Political Consequences

The Chakma and Hajongs do not fall into any of the above categories. They are not processed under UNHCR, nor are they subject to temporary asylum policies like Tibetan refugees. This is a crucial point that invalidates any claim that Chakma and Hajongs are conventional refugees. If they were, they would be part of an international system of refugee protection rather than an internal legal and administrative structure of India.

Additionally, the Indian government has never placed Chakma and Hajongs under UNHCR's mandate. Unlike recognized refugee groups, they do not depend on refugee-specific aid, resettlement programs, or asylum processes. Instead, Chakma and Hajongs have moved beyond the scope of refugee status and are now part of India's governance framework, unlike Tibetans, who remain on the periphery of citizenship.

Conclusion: Beyond the Refugee Label

Refugee status is not just a label—it is a legal condition that carries profound implications for an individual's rights, protections, and limitations within a host country. The Chakma and Hajongs' absence from UNHCR's Refugee Status Determination process, their possession of Indian identity documents, and their participation in civic life unequivocally demonstrate that they do not fit the conventional definition of refugees.

To continue labelling Chakma and Hajongs as refugees is a misrepresentation of their legal and social standing. Their status in India is not one of asylum-seekers awaiting protection but of a people who have integrated into the nation's framework. The distinction between Chakma and Hajongs and Tibetan refugees is clear: the former have moved beyond refugee status, while the latter remain bound by it. This legal and administrative reality must be acknowledged to ensure fair and accurate representation of the Chakma and Hajongs' rightful place in India.

Table: Comparison of Chakma & Hajongs vs. Tibetan Refugees in India – Why Chakma & Hajongs are not Refugees

Sl.	Features	Chakma & Hajongs	Tibetan Refugees
1	Land Ownership	Chakma & Hajongs were allotted 5 acres per family, recorded in the Chitta Record of Land, proving legal ownership.	Tibetan Refugees are only allotted land on lease for 20 years, which must be renewed periodically.
2	Place of Residence	Chakma & Hajongs live in recognized census villages under the Indian administrative framework.	Tibetan Refugees live in designated Tibetan refugee camps across India, such as Dharamshala (Himachal Pradesh), Bylakuppe & Mundgod (Karnataka),

			Dehradun (Uttarakhand), Tezu & Miao (Arunachal Pradesh), etc.
3	Dependent on International Aid	Chakma & Hajongs do not depend on international aid or grants from UNHCR or other humanitarian agencies.	Tibetan Refugees rely on international aid and receive grants from international humanitarian agencies.
4	Separate Rehabilitation Policy	There is no separate rehabilitation policy for Chakma & Hajongs.	Tibetan Refugees have a separate Tibetan Rehabilitation Policy, 2014, under the Ministry of Home Affairs (MHA).
5	Administration	Chakma & Hajongs are governed by local Indian administration, subject to Indian laws and governance structures.	Tibetan Refugees are governed by the Freedom Fighters & Rehabilitation (FFR) wing of MHA, in coordination with the Central Tibetan Administration (CTA) (Tibetan Government-in-Exile), the Central Tibetan Relief Committee (CTRC) (Governing Body for Settlements), and Tibetan Settlements' Local

			Governance & Administration.[36]
6	Population Census	Chakma & Hajongs are included in India's official decadal census conducted by the Government of India.	Tibetan Refugees are not included in India's official census, as they are classified as foreigners/refugees. Their population census is conducted by the Central Tibetan Administration (CTA), with some monitoring by the Indian government.
7	Foreigners Act, 1946	Chakma & Hajongs are not refugees and are not tracked under the Foreigners Act, 1946.	Tibetan Refugees are classified as foreigners/refugees and are tracked separately from Indian citizens under the Foreigners Act, 1946.
8	Voting Rights	As of 2024, 9,300 Chakma & Hajongs are enrolled in India's electoral rolls and can vote in Assembly	Tibetan Refugees do not have voting rights in India, as they are classified as foreigners/refugees.

		and Parliamentary Elections (but not in Panchayat elections)	
9	Identity Documents	Chakma & Hajongs possess Indian identity documents, including Voter ID (EPIC), Passport, Aadhaar Card, PAN Card, and Driving License.	Tibetan Refugees are issued Registration Certificates (RCs), which act as their identity documents. They must renew their RCs every five years, allowing India to track their presence.
10	UNHCR Refugee Status Determination	Chakma & Hajongs are not recognized as refugees by UNHCR and are not covered under UNHCR's Refugee Status Determination (RSD) process.	Tibetan Refugees are recognized as refugees under UNHCR's Refugee Status Determination (RSD) process, which grants them refugee status.

2

THE CITIZENSHIP DEBATE – MYTHS AND REALITIES

Persons (Chakma & Hajongs) settled in Arunachal Pradesh after their migration in 1964 but before the 1986 amendment of the Citizenship Act would be citizens of India.

- Ministry of Home Affairs

The citizenship of the Chakma and Hajongs of Arunachal Pradesh remains one of the most tragically misunderstood chapters in India's modern socio-political narrative. For decades, a fog of misinformation has shrouded their identity, reducing them to the derogatory label of "refugees" and stripping them of their rightful place as Indian citizens. This is not a mere misunderstanding—it is a wound, deliberately kept open by political agendas, administrative apathy, and a refusal to confront inconvenient truths. Far from being outsiders, the Chakma and Hajongs are woven into the fabric of Arunachal Pradesh, their roots planted deep in its soil through generations of birth and belonging. Yet, the myth of their "refugeehood" persists, a stubborn shadow that obscures their legal and moral claim to Indian citizenship.

As we unravel this tangled web in the pages that follow, one truth emerges with piercing clarity: the Chakma and Hajongs do not fit the refugee mold—neither by law nor by lived reality. This chapter seeks to shatter the myth once and for all, anchoring their citizenship in the unassailable framework of the Citizenship Act of 1955. Through a meticulous dissection of their generational composition, legal rights, and the forces that conspire to deny them, we will illuminate a story of resilience, injustice, and an unshakable claim to identity. The Chakma and Hajongs are not asking for charity; they are demanding what is theirs by birth and by right.

2.1. UNDERSTANDING THE GENERATIONAL COMPOSITION OF CHAKMA & HAJONGS

To grasp the citizenship debate with clarity, we must first see the Chakma and Hajongs not as a monolith but as a community defined by two distinct generational threads—each with its own legal standing, each a testament to their deep ties to India. These categories are not academic trivia; they are the beating heart of the Chakma and Hajongs' claim to citizenship, a distinction that holds the key to dismantling decades of falsehoods.

Category-A: The Original Migrant Chakma & Hajongs (1964–1969): These are the pioneers, the Chakma and Hajongs who arrived in NEFA (now Arunachal Pradesh) between 1964 and 1969, not as infiltrators but as part of a deliberate government resettlement program. Uprooted from their ancestral homes, Hajongs due to communal violence in the Mymensing District and Chakma in the Chittagong Hill Tracts due to the Kaptai Dam's devastating floods, they were offered sanctuary in India—a promise of a new beginning under the Indian state's protective wing. Today, they form a mere 5% of the Chakma and Hajong population in Arunachal Pradesh, their numbers dwindling as time claims the elders among them.

In 1997, 4,637 of these original migrants took a bold step toward formal recognition, applying for citizenship under Section 5 of the Citizenship Act, 1955—Citizenship by Registration[37]. They met every legal criterion, their lives already intertwined with India's

---

[37] *Section 5(1) in The Citizenship Act, 1955,*
https://indiankanoon.org/doc/1860219/

destiny for over three decades. Yet, the government's response was silence—a bureaucratic betrayal that left their applications gathering dust. By 2018, the toll of this neglect was stark: 539 applications had vanished, 915 applicants had passed away, and one form lay mutilated. Of the 1,798 [38] still alive and seeking citizenship, many have since joined their ancestors, their dreams of recognition extinguished by the state's indifference. This is not a technical delay; it is a quiet violence, a refusal to honour a promise made long ago.

Category-B: The Indigenous-born Chakma and Hajongs [Descendants of the Category-A (Original Migrants)]: Here lies the soul of the Chakma community—95% of its population, born not in some distant land but on the very soil of Arunachal Pradesh. These are the sons and daughters, grandchildren and great-grandchildren of the original migrants (Category-a), their births a living testament to their belonging. Under the Citizenship Act of 1955, Section 3 (1) (a) anyone born in India before July 1, 1987, is an Indian citizen by birth, irrespective of their parents' origins [39]. For the vast majority of Chakma and Hajongs, this is not a privilege to be granted—it is a right they inherited the moment they drew their first breath on Indian ground.

Their citizenship is not a theory; it is a fact, etched into the law and affirmed by their lives. Yet, the state government's recognition of this truth has been grudging at best. When the Chakma and Hajongs first secured voting rights in 2004, only 1,497 were enrolled—a paltry fraction of their numbers. By the 2024 Assembly and Parliamentary elections, electoral rolls listed just 9,300 [40]Chakma

---

[38] *Report Submitted by the Member Secretary, Aruanachal Pradesh State Legal Service Authority, Itanagar in Supreme Court Case WP(C) No. 510 of 2007, https://www.sci.gov.in/case-status-case-no/*
[39] *The Citizenship Act, 1955, Citizenship by birth, https://www.indiacode.nic.in/bitstream/123456789/6793/1/the_citizen ship_act_1955.pdf*
[40] *Electoral Roll, Arunachal Pradesh: https://ceoarunachal.nic.in/*

and Hajong voters out of an estimated 35,000 eligible citizens across three constituencies. This means that over 70% of eligible Chakma and Hajong voters remain excluded, their voices silenced not by law but by a system that refuses to see them. These are not statistics—they are the faces of a people yearning to be counted, to belong fully in the land of their birth.

Why Categorization Matters: The Line Between Truth and Deception

The distinction between the Original Migrant Chakma and Hajongs (Category-A) and the Indigenous-born Chakma (Category-B) is not a mere footnote—it is the fulcrum on which the entire citizenship debate turns. To blur these lines, as the state and its allies so often do, is to perpetuate a lie that robs the Chakma-Hajong people of their dignity. The original migrants, though few, deserve the citizenship they sought, their applications a plea for justice rooted in decades of contribution to Arunachal Pradesh. The indigenous-born, the overwhelming majority, need no such plea—their citizenship is a birthright, as Indian as the mountains that cradle their homes.

Yet, this vital distinction is routinely ignored. Academia clings to outdated narratives, scholars too timid or too complicit to revisit the Chakma and Hajongs' status in light of legal evolution. The state government, meanwhile, wields this confusion as a weapon, lumping all Chakma and Hajongs under the "migrant" or "refugee" banner to justify their exclusion. By focusing on the 5% whose citizenship applications languish, the administration obscures the 95% who need no certificate to call India home. This is not an oversight—it is a strategy, a deliberate muddling of waters to keep the Chakma and Hajongs in limbo.

The Deliberate Confusion: A Political and Administrative Sin

The state government's playbook is as cynical as it is effective. By refusing to process the citizenship applications applied in 1997 of the original migrants (Category-A), it creates a convenient smokescreen—a technicality to question the entire community's legitimacy. By ignoring the birthright of the indigenous-born (Category-B), it fuels a narrative of "outsiderhood" that resonates with political groups like the All Arunachal Pradesh Students' Union (AAPSU), media outlets hungry for division, and academics too lazy to challenge the status quo. This is not confusion born of complexity; it is confusion engineered to oppress, to deny the Chakma-Hajong people their place at the home they built.

The stakes of this misclassification are profound. It strips the Chakma and Hajongs of their electoral power, their access to education, their right to livelihoods—all the privileges of citizenship they are entitled to enjoy. It casts them as perpetual foreigners in their own land, a stigma that seeps into every facet of their lives. To club the two groups together is to erase the truth of their story, to silence the voices of the 95% whose citizenship is beyond dispute.

Categorization as Liberation: Rewriting the Narrative

The path to justice begins with seeing the Chakma and Hajongs as they are: two groups, united by history but distinct in their legal claims. The original migrants (Category-A) deserve the dignity of citizenship long promised and unjustly withheld. The indigenous-born (Category-B) demand recognition not as an act of grace but as an acknowledgment of their inalienable rights. To honour this distinction is to tear down the scaffolding of lies that has propped up the "refugee" myth for far too long.

This is more than a legal battle—it is a moral reckoning. The Chakma and Hajongs of Arunachal Pradesh are not shadows lurking at India's margins; they are its children, their lives a testament to endurance and hope. To deny them their citizenship and rights as citizens is to betray the very ideals of a nation built on justice and inclusion. Let us end this chapter of shame—not with platitudes, but with a clarion call: **the Chakma and Hajongs are Indian, by law, by birth, by right.** It is time the world, and Arunachal Pradesh, saw them as such. Their fight is not for a favour—it is for a truth that can no longer be suppressed.

2.2. SETTLED BY COURT OF LAW: CHAKMA AND HAJONGS ARE CITIZENS

The story of the Chakma and Hajongs of Arunachal Pradesh is one steeped in resilience, yet shadowed by a persistent and baseless myth: that they are not citizens of India. This question, which should have faded into irrelevance decades ago, was decisively settled by the year 2000, when a landmark court ruling affirmed their voting rights and, by extension, their citizenship[41]. Yet, despite the weight of legal clarity, judicial pronouncements, and the government's own admissions, a fog of doubt continues to swirl around their status—perpetuated not by evidence, but by political agendas and exclusionary rhetoric. It is time to dismantle this myth with the force of truth, to shine a light on the Chakma and Hajongs' rightful place in the Indian tapestry, and to honor the law that has long recognized them as citizens.

Legal Bedrock: Citizenship by Birth, Anchored in the Citizenship Act, 1955

---

[41] *Landmark Judgement on Election Law (A compilation of important Judgements prounced by the Supreme Court of India, High Courts and Election Commision of India, Volume-V) Delhi High Court WP (C) No. 886 of 2000, PUCL & CCRCAP vs Election Commission of India and PIL No. 52 of 2010 (AAPSU vs ECI)*
https://ceodelhi.gov.in/WriteReadData/Landmark%20Judgments/LandmarkJudgementsVOLI.pdf

The foundation of the Chakma and Hajongs' citizenship is not a matter of debate or interpretation—it is a matter of law, etched into the very framework of India's legal system. Section 3 (1) (a) of the Citizenship Act, 1955, is unequivocal: **every person born in India on or after January 26, 1950, but before July 1, 1987, is a citizen of India by birth, irrespective of their parents' nationality** [42]. For the Chakma and Hajongs, who arrived in India in 1964 fleeing persecution in what was then East Pakistan, this provision is their shield and their right. Their children, born on Indian soil, grew up breathing the air of this nation, their lives intertwined with its soil and spirit. To question their citizenship is to question the very letter of the law that defines who belongs to India.

Armed with this constitutional guarantee, the Chakma and Hajongs took their fight to the courts. In 2000, they filed a petition in the Delhi High Court [39]—not to beg for recognition, but to demand what was already theirs: inclusion in the electoral rolls of Arunachal Pradesh. Their plea was not a cry for charity; it was a call for justice, rooted in the unassailable truth of their birthright.

The Government's Own Words: An Affidavit That Silenced Doubt

The response to their petition was nothing short of a revelation. The Central Government itself, in an affidavit submitted to the Delhi High Court, laid bare the reality of the Chakma and Hajongs' status. With clarity that cut through decades of obfuscation, the affidavit declared: *"Persons (Chakma & Hajongs) settled in Arunachal Pradesh after their migration in 1964 but before the 1986 amendment of the Citizenship Act would be citizens of India."* This was not a reluctant concession or a vague suggestion—it was an official, binding recognition of the Chakma and Hajongs as Indian citizens. The

---

[42] *Government of India. (1955). The Citizenship Act, 1955.* *https://legislative.gov.in/*

government, the ultimate arbiter of legal identity, had spoken. Any lingering ambiguity was swept away, leaving only the truth: the Chakma and Hajongs belong to India, as much as any other citizen born within its borders.

Enfranchisement: Voting Rights as Living Proof

The court's ruling that followed was not just a legal victory—it was a resounding affirmation of the Chakma and Hajongs' place in India's democracy. Voting rights, the cornerstone of citizenship, were granted to them, a tangible recognition of their status. In 2004, the first wave of 1,497 Chakma and Hajongs stepped into polling booths across Arunachal Pradesh, casting their ballots in Parliamentary and State Assembly elections as proud Indian citizens. That number has since swelled, a testament to their growing presence and unshakable resolve. By the 2024 elections, 9,300 Chakma and Hajongs were enrolled as voters, their voices echoing through the democratic process—an irrefutable marker of their citizenship.

Yet, even as they exercised this fundamental right, the shadow of doubt persisted. The State Government and certain political factions, driven by narrow interests, continued to peddle the fiction that the Chakma and Hajongs are outsiders. Ignoring the Citizenship Act, the Central Government's affidavit, and the Delhi High Court's ruling, they clung to an exclusionary narrative, painting the Chakma and Hajongs as interlopers to justify denying them basic rights. This is not a legal dispute—it is a deliberate distortion, a calculated effort to erase the Chakma and Hajongs' identity and dignity.

Beyond the Law: A Human Truth

The Chakma and Hajongs are not a footnote in India's story— they are a living chapter, written in the sweat of their labor, the courage of their journey, and the hope of their children. To question their citizenship is to deny the spirit of a nation that prides itself on diversity and refuge. It is to turn a blind eye to the law that protects them, the courts that uphold them, and the votes they cast as equals. The evidence is overwhelming: the Citizenship Act enshrined their rights, the government affirmed them, and the ballot box sealed them. The myth of their non-citizenship is not just baseless—it is a betrayal of justice itself.

A Powerful Reckoning

It is time to end this manufactured controversy, to silence the voices that seek to divide rather than unite. The Chakma and Hajongs of Arunachal Pradesh are not asking for permission to belong—they are claiming what the law, the courts, and their very existence have already granted them. Their citizenship is not a privilege to be debated; it is a fact to be celebrated. Let the doubters be drowned out by the truth, let the naysayers be humbled by the law, and let the Chakma and Hajongs stand tall as full-fledged citizens of India—because that is who they are, and that is who they will always be. The myth is dead; the reality endures.

2.3. CITIZENS IN LAW, BUT NOT IN PRACTICE: THE SYSTEMATIC DENIAL OF RIGHTS TO CHAKMA AND HAJONGS

The Chakma and Hajongs of Arunachal Pradesh stand as a glaring testament to the chasm between legal entitlement and lived reality. Despite 95% of them being Indian citizens by birth under Section 3(1)(a) of the Citizenship Act, 1955, and the remaining 5%—the original migrant settlers of 1964–1969—having a Supreme Court-backed claim to citizenship under Section 5(1)(a), the community is trapped in a state-orchestrated limbo of exclusion. This is not mere bureaucratic oversight; it is a deliberate, systemic denial of rights that has relegated the Chakma and Hajongs to a sub-human existence, stripped of dignity, opportunity, and agency. The state government's refusal to recognize their citizenship in practice has entrenched generational disadvantage, perpetuating a cycle of poverty, marginalization, and despair. Far from being an isolated issue, this is a calculated assault on a vulnerable population, exposing the hollowness of India's constitutional promises of equality and justice.

The consequences of this non-recognition are profound and multifaceted, cutting across every sphere of life. Consider the following:

a) Denial of Identity and Domicile Documentation: The absence of basic identity documents—birth certificates, domicile certificates [43], or Scheduled Tribe status—effectively renders Chakma and Hajongs second class citizens in practice. This exclusion bars them from government welfare schemes, public sector jobs, and even private employment requiring formal identification. Without these documents, they are ghosts in their own country, unable to prove their existence or claim their rights.

b) Exclusion from Local Governance: The deliberate omission of Chakma and Hajongs from the Panchayati Raj system is a masterstroke of political disenfranchisement. By keeping them out of Gram Sabhas and Panchayat elections, the state ensures they have no voice in local decision-making, no stake in economic development, and no access to social justice mechanisms. This exclusion is not accidental—it is a strategic move to keep the community invisible and powerless.

c) Food Insecurity as Policy: Denied ration cards and access to the Public Distribution System (PDS) under the National Food

---

[43] *National Human Rights Commission (NHRC). (n.d.). Reports on the Status of Chakma in Arunachal Pradesh.* *https://nhrc.nic.in/*

Security Act [44], Chakma and Hajong families are denied food security. In a nation that prides itself on food security programs, this exclusion is a damning indictment of state prejudice, leaving entire households to fend for themselves in a system rigged against them.

d) Educational Apartheid: Chakma and Hajong students are systematically locked out of scholarship schemes like the Pre-Matric and Post-Matric Scholarships for Minorities and the Merit Cum Means Scholarship for Professional and Technical Courses [45]—fully funded Central Sector Schemes sabotaged by state-level gatekeeping. Applications are rejected at the authorization stage, a clear abuse of administrative power that robs Chakma youth of educational mobility and perpetuates illiteracy and poverty.

e) Healthcare as a Privilege, Not a Right: Exclusion from flagship programs like the Pradhan Mantri Jan Arogya Yojana (AB PM-JAY) [46] and the Chief Minister Arogya Arunachal Yojana (CMAAY) [47] leaves Chakma and Hajongs without access to affordable medical care. Families are driven into crippling debt or forced to forgo treatment altogether, turning basic healthcare into an unattainable luxury and exposing the state's callous disregard for their well-being.

f) Selective Welfare Blockade: While some Central schemes trickle through, state-implemented programs—especially those routed through Panchayati Raj Institutions—are withheld. Housing, employment, women's empowerment, rural development, and skill

---

[44] *Government of India. (2013). The National Food Security Act, 2013.* *https://dfpd.gov.in/*

[45] *Ministry of Minority Affairs. (n.d.). Pre-Matric and Post-Matric Scholarships for Minorities. https://minorityaffairs.gov.in/*

[46] *Ministry of Health and Family Welfare. (n.d.). Pradhan Mantri Jan Arogya Yojana (PM-JAY). https://pmjay.gov.in/*

[47] *Government of Arunachal Pradesh. (n.d.). Chief Minister Arogya Arunachal Yojana (CMAAY). https://cmaay.com/*

training remain out of reach, ensuring that Chakma and Hajongs are perpetually sidelined from the benefits of governance.

g) Economic Strangulation: The refusal to issue trading licenses stifles Chakma and Hajong entrepreneurship, barring them from starting businesses or engaging in trade. This economic chokehold traps the community in stagnation, with no pathway to self-reliance or prosperity.

h) Educational Neglect: Government schools in Chakma and Hajong areas are plagued by staff shortages, crumbling infrastructure, and outdated resources. The absence of colleges forces students to either abandon their education or migrate out of state at prohibitive costs—a choice most cannot afford, consigning them to a future of limited horizons.

i) Landlessness and Abandonment: Repeated floods have eroded vast swathes of Chakma farmland, yet the state offers no rehabilitation or support. Displaced families are left to toil as tenant farmers under exploitative landlords, their plight ignored by a government that seems content to let them sink deeper into distress.

j) Child Exploitation as a Symptom: Economic desperation drives Chakma families to send their children to well-off families as domestic workers, where they face verbal, physical, and sexual abuse—or worse, vanish into trafficking networks [48]. This is not a mere tragedy; it is a direct consequence of state neglect that has turned minors into collateral damage.

k) A Generation Lost to Despair: With no jobs, no higher education, and no prospects, Chakma and Hajong youth are increasingly ensnared by drug addiction and alcoholism. This rising

---

[48] *'Bhonti culture': How minor girls from Assam are sold into slavery in Arunachal Pradesh by Maitreyee Boruah,*
https://thefederal.com/category/the-eighth-column/bhonti-culture-how-minor-girls-from-assam-are-sold-into-slavery-in-arunachal-pradesh-98342

tide of substance abuse is not a moral failing—it is a predictable outcome of a system that offers them nothing but hopelessness.

l) Institutional Hostility: In government offices and public institutions, Chakma and Hajongs encounter routine harassment, rudeness, and outright refusal of services. This institutional discrimination is not an aberration but a normalized tactic to alienate and dehumanize them further.

The Chakma and Hajongs' plight is a stark reminder that citizenship on paper is meaningless without its practical enforcement. The Arunachal Pradesh government's actions—or inactions—constitute a sustained violation of constitutional rights, defying both the letter of the law and the spirit of justice. The Supreme Court's directives have been flouted, legal entitlements ignored, and an entire community left to languish in a state of engineered deprivation. This is not just a failure of governance; it is a betrayal of India's democratic ethos, demanding urgent redress through judicial intervention, policy reform, and accountability for those perpetuating this injustice. The Chakma and Hajongs are citizens in law—high time they are treated as such in practice.

2.4. MISINFORMATION AND MANIPULATION OF TRUTH AS STATE GOVERNMENT POLICY: THE CHAKMA & HAJONG CITIZENSHIP ISSUE

Despite being citizens by law, the Chakma and Hajongs in Arunachal Pradesh face systematic denial of their rights, institutional discrimination, exclusion from welfare schemes, and political invisibility. This is not a mere administrative oversight, but a deliberate policy of misinformation and manipulation orchestrated by the state government and the All Arunachal Pradesh Students' Union (AAPSU). By hiding the truth about Chakma and Hajongs citizenship status, controlling narratives through political and media propaganda, and exploiting technical and legal loopholes, these powerful entities sustain a false perception that Chakma and Hajongs are outsiders or illegal migrants. This strategy results in their systematic exclusion from political representation and rights, with severe consequences for the community. Breaking this cycle requires legal enforcement, narrative correction, and a critical re-examination by researchers, scholars, and academia to restore justice and uphold the Chakma and Hajongs' rightful status as Indian citizens.

Below, I critically analyse how this manipulation unfolds, its consequences, and the urgent need for change.

a) Hiding the Truth About Chakma & Hajong Citizenship

The Chakma, an ethnic group originally from the Chittagong Hill Tracts and Hajongs from Mymensing District in erstwhile East Pakistan (now Bangladesh), migrated to India—particularly Arunachal Pradesh—in the 1960s due to displacement caused by the Kaptai Dam and political unrest. Today, **95% of Chakma and Hajongs in Arunachal Pradesh are citizens by birth** [49] under Section 3 of the Citizenship Act, 1955, which considers anyone born in India (a)on or after the 26th day of January, 1950, but before the 1st day of July, 1987 . However, the state government and AAPSU systematically suppress this legal reality in public discourse.

- **Blurring Legal Distinctions**: Authorities deliberately conflate the original migrant Chakma and Hajongs (who arrived between 1964-1969) with their descendants, who are indisputably citizens by birth. This confusion muddies the waters, allowing officials to treat all Chakma and Hajongs as if their citizenship is in question.

---

[49] *The Core Idea – CRDO, https://crdo.chakma.in/crdo-the-core-idea/*

- **Denial of Documentation**: When Chakma and Hajongs apply for identity documents or government benefits, they face unnecessary demands to "prove" their citizenship—despite their legal status being automatic under the law. This bureaucratic hurdle perpetuates the myth that they are not citizens, hiding the truth from both the public and the Chakma and Hajongs themselves.

This deliberate obfuscation serves to maintain the Chakma and Hajongs in a liminal state—legally Indian, yet practically stateless.

b) Controlling the Narrative Through Political and Media Propaganda

The state government and AAPSU wield significant influence over the political and media landscape in Arunachal Pradesh, using this power to propagate a misleading narrative that all Chakma and Hajong are "illegal immigrants."

- **Political Rhetoric**: AAPSU and regional political groups consistently label Chakma and Haongs as refugees, illegal immigrants and outsiders, framing them as a threat to indigenous identity and resources. This rhetoric is echoed by state officials, embedding the falsehood into official discourse.

- **Media Complicity**: Mainstream media outlets in the region uncritically reproduce this narrative, rarely questioning its legal or factual basis. Positive developments—such as the 2000 Delhi High Court judgment affirming Chakma and Hajongs as citizens by birth—are sidelined or ignored, ensuring the public remains misinformed.

- **Erasure of Legal Victories**: Even when courts uphold Chakma and Hajong rights, the dominant narrative drowns out these rulings. The lack of media amplification keeps the public perception skewed, reinforcing the idea that Chakma and Hajongs lack legitimacy.

This propaganda machine ensures that the Chakma and Hajongs remain vilified and misunderstood, their citizenship obscured by a relentless campaign of misinformation.

c) Weaponizing the Absence of Citizenship Certificates of original migrant Chakma & Hajongs

A key strategy in this manipulation is the state's exploitation of technical and legal loopholes, particularly concerning citizenship certificates for a small minority of Chakma and Hajongs. To understand this, we must distinguish between two groups within the Chakma and Hajong community in Arunachal Pradesh:

1. **Original Migrants (approximately 5% of the Chakma population)**: These individuals migrated to India between 1964 and 1969. Their citizenship applications remain pending due to deliberate delays by the state government.

2. **Descendants Born in India (approximately 95%)**: These Chakma and Hajongs were born in Arunachal Pradesh and are automatically citizens by birth under Section 3 of the Citizenship Act, 1955. They do not need citizenship certificates, as their status is legally secure.

- **Legal Acknowledgment Ignored**: The Ministry of Home Affairs (MHA) has confirmed in court that Chakma and Hajongs born in Arunachal Pradesh before 1986 are citizens by birth. This ruling applies to the 95% of Chakma and Hajongs born in India. However, the state government refuses to accept this legal fact and instead groups them with the original migrants (the 5%), creating confusion about their status.

- **Exploiting the Loophole**: The state government intentionally delays processing citizenship applications for the (Category-A) original migrants (5%). This inaction allows authorities to question the citizenship of all Chakma and Hajongs, including the 95% who are citizens by birth and need no certificates. The citizenship of those born in India is already proven by their possession of Indian identity documents, such as: Passports, Voter IDs (EPIC), Aadhaar cards, PAN cards, Driving licenses etc.

  Despite this evidence, the government lumps both groups together (Category-A & Category-B), casting doubt on the entire community's status whenever it suits their agenda.

- **Bureaucratic Obstructionism**: By refusing to process certificates for the original migrants and failing to recognize the legal citizenship of those born in India, the government perpetuates the false impression that all Chakma and Hajongs' citizenship is unresolved. In truth, the citizenship of the 95% born in India is firmly established under the law, requiring no further documentation.

This approach demonstrates how the state uses procedural delays and bureaucratic tactics to obscure a clear legal reality, trapping the Chakma and Hajong communities in a cycle of exclusion and denial of rights.

d) Systematic Exclusion from Political Representation and Rights

The false narrative that Chakma and Hajongs are not citizens directly justifies their systematic exclusion from political and social rights, rendering them powerless to challenge their marginalization.

- **Denial of Voting Rights**: Chakma and Hajongs are barred from voting in state's Panchayat elections or participating in local governance, such as Panchayati Raj institutions. Even when they gain voting rights in parliamentary and assembly elections, their exclusion from local level processes keeps them voiceless where it matters most.

- **Barriers to Employment and Welfare**: The lack of recognition prevents Chakma and Hajongs from accessing state government jobs, educational opportunities, healthcare, and welfare schemes reserved for citizens. This economic disenfranchisement reinforces their marginal status.

- **Perpetual Powerlessness**: Without political representation or access to governance structures, Chakma and Hajongs cannot advocate for their interests or counter the policies that oppress them. This exclusion ensures the false narrative remains unchallenged.

By stripping Chakma and Hajongs of practical rights, the state and AAPSU maintain their dominance, using misinformation as a tool to silence an entire community.

The Consequences of this False Narrative

The sustained campaign of misinformation has devastating effects on the Chakma and Hajong communities, creating a stark disconnect between their legal status and lived reality.

- **Legal Citizenship, No Practical Rights**: Despite being Indian citizens by law, Chakma and Hajongs face relentless barriers to documentation, employment, education, healthcare, and social welfare. Their citizenship exists on paper but not in practice.

- **Perpetual Disenfranchisement**: Exclusion from state-level political processes keeps Chakma and Hajongs voiceless, unable to influence the policies that govern their lives. This political invisibility perpetuates their vulnerability.

- **Sustained Marginalization and Discrimination**: The false narrative fuels xenophobia and anti-Chakma and Hajong sentiment among the broader population. Social discrimination, harassment, and institutional apathy become normalized, entrenching their second-class status.

This vicious cycle—where misinformation leads to exclusion, which in turn reinforces the misinformation—traps Chakma and Hajongs in a state of perpetual marginalization, denied the dignity and rights their citizenship should guarantee.

Breaking the Cycle of Misinformation and Restoring Justice

Ending this injustice demands a multi-faceted approach to dismantle the false narrative and restore Chakma rights.

- **Legal Enforcement and Policy Reforms**: The state and central governments must be held accountable for failing to uphold Chakma and Hajong's rights as citizens. Courts should mandate the issuance of documentation and access to benefits, closing the technical loopholes exploited by authorities.

- **Correcting the Narrative**: Scholars, researchers, activists, and independent media must counter the propaganda with facts, emphasizing the legal basis of Chakma and Hajong citizenship and amplifying their court victories. Public awareness campaigns can shift societal perceptions.

- **Demanding Equal Rights and Representation**: The Chakma and Hajong communities, supported by allies, must push for full inclusion in governance, recognition of their status, and an end to systemic discrimination. Political mobilization is key to breaking their enforced silence.

The Role of Researchers, Scholars, and Academia

Academia has a pivotal role in this struggle, moving beyond outdated frameworks to re-contextualize and re-interpret the Chakma issue.

- **Reframing the Chakma and Hajong Narrative**: Chakma and Hajongs should no longer be studied as refugees or stateless individuals — a mischaracterization that aligns with the state's propaganda. Instead, they must be recognized as a distinct category: **legally recognized citizens who are systematically disenfranchised**. This This shift exposes the state's role in their exclusion and challenges the false narrative at its root.

- **Investigating State Power**: Researchers can explore how state-level executive authority undermines citizenship rights, using the Chakma and Hajong case as a lens to understand broader issues of citizenship and exclusion in India. Comparative studies with other marginalized groups could further illuminate these dynamics.

- **Bridging Law and Reality**: Scholars should analyse the discrepancy between central laws (like the Citizenship Act) and state-level implementation, highlighting how bureaucratic discretion is weaponized to deny rights.

By producing rigorous, evidence-based critiques, academia can provide the intellectual foundation for policy reform and public advocacy, ensuring the Chakma and Hajongs' status as Indian citizens is upheld in practice, not just in theory.

3

ARE CHAKMA AND HAJONGS ILLEGALLY REHABILITATED IN ARUNACHAL PRADESH?

The question of whether the Chakma and Hajongs are illegally rehabilitated in Arunachal Pradesh has been at the heart of socio-political discourse in the state for decades. This narrative, frequently invoked by political leaders—particularly during election campaigns—and aggressively championed by the All–Arunachal Pradesh Students' Union (AAPSU), has played a crucial role in shaping public opinion against the Chakma and Hajong communities.

The power of repetition in constructing public perception cannot be underestimated. As the infamous propaganda principle attributed to Joseph Goebbels states, *"Repeat a lie often enough, and it becomes the truth."* Over time, the claim that the Chakma and Hajongs are illegal settlers has become so deeply ingrained in public consciousness that it is often accepted as an unquestionable fact. This persistent repetition has created what psychologists call the *"illusion of truth"*— where misinformation, repeated long enough, starts appearing credible despite lacking factual accuracy.

The Core of the Accusation

The central arguments propagated by AAPSU and certain political groups regarding the Chakma and Hajongs' presence in Arunachal Pradesh are as follows:

i) Chakma and Hajongs are illegally settled in Arunachal Pradesh, allegedly in violation of the Bengal Eastern Frontier

Regulation Act of 1873, which mandates an Inner Line Permit (ILP) for non-native Indians entering the state.

ii) The indigenous people of Arunachal Pradesh were not consulted before the Chakma and Hajongs were settled in the state, implying an undemocratic imposition by external authorities meaning the central government.

iii) The illegal migration of Chakma and Hajong persists at such a concerning level that it threatens to diminish the indigenous population to a minority.

At first glance, these allegations may seem compelling, especially when repeated over generations. However, a closer examination of historical records, government policies, and legal precedents reveals an entirely different reality.

Challenging the False Narrative

A major legal development that undermines AAPSU's longstanding claims is its own litigation. In 2010, AAPSU filed a Public Interest Litigation (PIL) in the Gauhati High Court, challenging the Chakma and Hajongs' settlement in Arunachal Pradesh. The legal proceedings and judicial responses to this case expose the fallacies within the widely accepted narrative.

In this chapter, we will dissect and debunk these misrepresentations by presenting historical facts, government records, and the wisdom of Indian courts. Through an evidence-based approach, we aim to correct the distorted discourse and bring to light the legal and ethical realities concerning the Chakma and Hajongs communities settlement and rehabilitation in Arunachal Pradesh.

3.1. JUDICIAL CLARITY: THE GAUHATI HIGH COURT'S STANCE ON ALLEGED ILLEGAL CHAKMA AND HAJONG'S SETTLEMENT

One of the most significant legal challenges to the Chakma and Hajong community's settlement in Arunachal Pradesh came in 2010 when the All–Arunachal Pradesh Students' Union (AAPSU) filed a Public Interest Litigation (PIL No. 52 of 2010) in the Gauhati High Court. In their petition, AAPSU contended that the Chakma and Hajongs' settlement in the state was illegal as it allegedly contravened colonial-era regulations such as the Bengal Eastern Frontier Regulation (BEFR) Act of 1873 [50] and the Chin Hills Regulation of 1896. Consequently, they argued that Chakma and Hajongs should not be considered ordinary residents of Arunachal Pradesh and, therefore, should not be eligible to vote in the state's elections.

AAPSU's Arguments in Court

AAPSU's legal challenge was based on a key claim: **Violation of the Bengal Eastern Frontier Regulation (BEFR), 1873** – The BEFR imposes restrictions on the entry of non-indigenous individuals into designated "excluded" areas, mandating an Inner Line Permit (ILP) for access. AAPSU contended that since the Chakma and Hajongs did not possess ILPs, their settlement in Arunachal Pradesh was unlawful, rendering them ineligible to be recognized as ordinary residents or included in the state's electoral roll. [51]

a) The Gauhati High Court's Verdict: A Clear Rebuttal

After examining the case, the Gauhati High Court on 19 March 2013 firmly dismissed AAPSU's claims. The court ruled that the Chakma and Hajongs' settlement in Arunachal Pradesh was a

---

[50] *What is Bengal Eastern Frontier Regulation in 1873,*
https://eilp.arunachal.gov.in/actDetails
[51] *https://hcservices.ecourts.gov.in/*

legitimate policy decision taken by the Government of India in consultation with the then authorities of Arunachal Pradesh (NEFA). Therefore, the argument that their settlement violated the BEFR was legally untenable [52].

The key points in the court's ruling were:

- **No Violation of BEFR (1873)** – The Court clarified that once the Government of India had officially settled the Chakma and Hajongs in Arunachal Pradesh, they were deemed residents of the state and did not require an Inner Line Permit.

- **Recognition as Residents** – The ruling stated that Chakma and Hajongs, having been settled with the approval of the government, had acquired the status of legal residents of Arunachal Pradesh.

- **Government's Sovereign Decision** – The Court reaffirmed that the decision to settle the Chakma and Hajongs was a sovereign policy decision, and challenging it decades later on the basis of colonial-era regulations was legally and morally flawed.

The Significance of the Verdict

This judgment not only exposed the inaccuracies in AAPSU's claims but also reinforced the legal basis of the Chakma and Hajongs' settlement in Arunachal Pradesh. The PIL had aimed to challenge the Chakma and Hajongs' right to residence and electoral participation, but instead, it led to a judicial validation of their legal status.

Despite this clear judicial pronouncement, the misinformation continues to be propagated in political and public discourse,

---

[52] *The Gauhati High Court, PIL No. 52 of 2010, Case Details:* *https://hcservices.ecourts.gov.in*

demonstrating how deeply entrenched false narratives can be. However, legal precedent stands firm: The Chakma and Hajongs were settled lawfully, and their residence in Arunachal Pradesh is not illegal.

b) Official Recognition: The Chakma and Hajongs as Legal Migrants, Not Illegal Settlers

The Chakma and Hajong people who migrated to India in 1964 were not illegal infiltrators but registered refugees who were formally recognized and rehabilitated by the Government of India. They were issued Relief and Rehabilitation (R&R) certificates and were resettled in the North Eastern Frontier Agency (NEFA), now Arunachal Pradesh, under a structured rehabilitation program spanning from 1964 to 1969. This was not an arbitrary or illegal settlement, but a planned, government-sponsored initiative aimed at providing a permanent home to these displaced communities.

Initially, the Chakma and Hajongs had were placed in transit camps in Assam awaiting final rehabilitation before being relocated to NEFA (Arunachal Pradesh), which at that time was administratively and constitutionally a part of Assam. The migration and settlement were conducted with the full knowledge, consultation and approval of the central and state authorities.

3.2. THE LEGAL STATUS OF CHAKMA AND HAJONG REHABILITATION: CLARITY FROM OFFICIAL RECORDS

For years after their settlement, the legality of Chakma and Hajong rehabilitation was not questioned. However, in the 1980s, as political rhetoric against the community intensified, the issue of their legal status was raised. In response, numerous official communications between the Government of Arunachal Pradesh and the Government of India reaffirmed that the Chakma and Hajongs were legal migrants, not illegal settlers.

Some of the key official references that confirm the Chakma and Hajongs' legal migration include:

(a) Official Clarification by the Ministry of Rehabilitation (February 16, 1982)

In a high-level meeting attended by then-Chief Minister Gegong Apang, state ministers of Arunachal Pradesh, and representatives from the Ministry of Home Affairs (MHA), **Mr. R.N. Hota, Joint Secretary, Ministry of Rehabilitation,** provided a categorical clarification on the Chakma and Hajongs' status. He stated:

- The Chakma were brought to Arunachal Pradesh in 1964-65 by the Government of India and were not infiltrators.
- Unlike post-1971 Bangladeshi infiltrators, the Chakma were officially recognized and settled by the government through a structured rehabilitation program.[53]

(b) Statement by Shri B.P. Mishra, Deputy Secretary, Ministry of Home Affairs (1982)

In the same meeting, Shri B.P. Mishra, Deputy Secretary, MHA, made an important distinction between illegal migrants in Assam and the settled Chakma in Arunachal Pradesh:

- The Chakma were officially registered refugees, unlike the unregulated Bangladeshi infiltrators in Assam.
- Their migration and settlement were monitored, approved, and facilitated by the Government of India.

---

[53] *The National Archives of India – Ministry of Home Affairs File No. 13024/5/73AP Volume-III (Correspondence) Subject: Settlement of Chakma in Arunachal Pradesh*

- Even Assam's political leadership acknowledged that these refugees were legitimately settled by the government.

(iii) Ministry of Home Affairs' Official Communication to the Prime Minister's Office (September 13, 1982)

The question of Chakma settlement in Arunachal Pradesh was formally addressed in a Ministry of Home Affairs (MHA) communication to the Prime Minister's Office (PMO) under UO No. 13024/5/73-AP(Vol.III). This official response explicitly dismissed allegations of illegal infiltration and reaffirmed that:

- There was no infiltration of foreigners in Arunachal Pradesh.
- The Chakma were settled under a well-defined rehabilitation scheme formulated and executed by the Ministry of Rehabilitation, Government of India.
- By 1982, the Chakma had already been residing in Arunachal Pradesh for nearly two decades, making the demand for their removal both legally and ethically untenable. [51]

This official stance directly contradicts claims that the Chakma entered Arunachal Pradesh illegally. Their settlement was not a case of unauthorized encroachment but a deliberate policy decision by the Indian government.

(iv) Parliamentary Discussion: Clarification in the Lok Sabha (August 5 & September 23, 1992)

The issue of Chakma settlement was formally raised in the Indian Parliament when Mr. Laeta Umbrey, Member of Parliament (MP) from Arunachal Pradesh, addressed concerns about their presence in the state.

- On August 5, 1992, Mr. Umbrey questioned the legal basis of Chakma settlement, expressing apprehensions similar to those raised by political groups in Arunachal Pradesh.
- In response, on September 23, 1992, Mr. M.M. Jacob, Minister of State for Home and Parliamentary Affairs, provided an authoritative clarification:
  - The Chakma' settlement in Arunachal Pradesh was not arbitrary but carefully planned by the Government of India.
  - The process was executed in full cooperation with the Arunachal Pradesh government, contradicting claims that the state authorities were unaware or uninvolved.
  - The rehabilitation effort was part of a structured national policy rather than an act of unauthorized settlement. [54]

This parliamentary clarification reinforces the fact that the Chakma and Hajongs' migration, settlement and rehabilitation in Arunachal Pradesh were carried out through legal channels and government approval at both central and state levels.

These official statements, along with multiple government records, clearly dispel the false narrative that Chakma and Hajongs are illegal settlers in Arunachal Pradesh. Their settlement was a deliberate, state-backed policy decision, not an act of unlawful encroachment.

Despite these facts, certain political groups continue to exploit misinformation for electoral and political gains, ignoring the documented truth that the Chakma and Hajongs were legally

---

[54] *M.M. Jacob, Minister of State for Home and Parliamentary Affairs, reply letter to Laeta Umbrey, Member of Parliament, Lok Sabha, D.O. No. 12/16/92-NE, 23 September 1992.*

migrated, settled, and rehabilitated in Arunachal Pradesh with full governmental approval.

The question, therefore, is not whether the Chakma and Hajongs are illegal settlers—it is why, despite overwhelming evidence to the contrary, this narrative continues to be propagated.

3.3. WERE THE INDIGENOUS PEOPLE CONSULTED BEFORE THE CHAKMA AND HAJONG SETTLEMENT?

One of the most persistent claims surrounding the Chakma and Hajong settlement in Arunachal Pradesh is that the indigenous people were not consulted before their rehabilitation, implying that the decision was an undemocratic imposition by the central government. However, official records and historical evidence contradict this narrative.

Multiple government documents, parliamentary discussions, and administrative correspondences confirm that local consultations did take place before the settlement of Chakma and Hajongs in designated areas. Below are key instances that dismantle the myth of unilateral imposition:

(a) Dr. Daying Ering's Recommendation & the Government's Response (May 1966)[55]

In May 1966, during a parliamentary delegation visit to NEFA (now Arunachal Pradesh), Dr. Daying Ering, then a Parliamentary Secretary, raised concerns about prior consultation and local consent before settling displaced communities like the Chakma. He

---

[55] *The National Archives of India – Ministry of Home Affairs NEFA Section File No. NE/463(22) Subject: Visit of Members of Parliament to NEFA in May 1966*

specifically pointed out potential issues in Nao-Dihing and Chowkham, advocating for local input in the decision-making process.

Government's Response:

- The Deputy Commissioners of the respective districts had already consulted local people, particularly those who had ancestral land claims in the proposed settlement areas.
- Nao-Dihing: The designated settlement land was part of the Diyun Reserved Forest, officially notified in 1951-52, making it government land. Since it had already been declared a Reserved Forest, no individual or community had hereditary ownership over it.
- Chowkham: The Khampti-Singpho Tribal Council had been consulted and gave consent for Chakma rehabilitation. Initially, they agreed to accommodate 1,000 families, but later requested a reduction to 200 families. The Government of India honoured their request and revised the scheme accordingly.

These documented instances prove that local consultations did happen, and tribal leadership was involved in key decisions regarding Chakma settlement.

(b) Union Home Minister's Letter to the Arunachal Pradesh CM (July 19, 1980)[56]

On July 19, 1980, Zail Singh, the then Home Minister of India, directly addressed the Chief Minister of Arunachal Pradesh, Gegong Apang, via an official letter (D.O. No.13024/5/73-AP.II).

---

[56] *The National Archives of India – Ministry of Home Affairs NEFA File No. 13024/5/73-AP. II Subject: Settlement of Chakma Refugees in Arunachal Pradesh*

Key Clarifications in the Letter:

- The Government of India's decision to settle Chakma was made after due consultation with the Arunachal Pradesh Administration.
- The Arunachal Pradesh government, in turn, consulted local leaders and communities before finalizing settlement sites.
- The settlement was not imposed unilaterally, as alleged, but was a structured decision taken in coordination with local administration and stakeholders.

This official communication from the highest levels of government negates the claim that local voices were ignored.

(c) 1982 Central Team Visit & Clarification by MHA (February 16, 1982)[57]

In February 1982, a Central Government team visited Arunachal Pradesh to review Chakma rehabilitation areas. During a meeting at the Chief Minister's residence, the Chief Minister of Arunachal Pradesh personally asked the team for a report on their findings and a clear statement on the policy of the Government of India regarding the Chakma.

Response by Shri B.P. Mishra, Deputy Secretary, Ministry of Home Affairs:

- He emphasized that the Chakma were not infiltrators, unlike certain groups in Assam.
- The Chakma had been registered as refugees in 1964 and were settled legally by the Government of India.

---

[57] *The National Archives of India – Ministry of Home Affairs NEFA File No. 13024/5/73-AP. II Subject: Settlement of Chakma Refugees in Arunachal Pradesh*

- Their rehabilitation was done with the knowledge and consent of the Arunachal Pradesh Administration at the time.
- The settlement process was deliberate, planned, and legal—not an act of arbitrary encroachment.

This statement by a senior MHA official reinforces that the Chakma' presence in Arunachal Pradesh was neither illegal nor imposed without local engagement.

Local Consultation Was Integral to the Chakma Settlement

Contrary to the widely circulated claim that the Chakma settlement was forced upon the indigenous population, historical records demonstrate that:

- *Local communities, including the Khampti-Singpho Tribal Council, were consulted before settlement areas were finalized.*

- *Arunachal Pradesh's administration played an active role in coordinating the settlement process with the central government.*

- *Official correspondences from both the Home Ministry and Prime Minister's Office affirm that proper procedures were followed.*

The misinformation surrounding the Chakma and Hajong settlement has been strategically used for political gains, fostering animosity and division between communities. However, the historical truth is clear: the Chakma and Hajongs were settled in Arunachal Pradesh through legal, structured, and consultative processes—not through unilateral imposition.

3.4. DEBUNKING THE MYTH OF ILLEGAL CHAKMA AND HAJONGS' MIGRATION: A CRITICAL EXAMINATION

The notion that the illegal migration of Chakma persists at such a concerning level that it threatens to diminish the indigenous population of Arunachal Pradesh to a minority is a baseless and fabricated narrative. This misleading claim is often amplified with exaggerated rhetoric to provoke fear and anxiety among indigenous communities, unjustly casting Chakma as infiltrators. The assertion hinges on the unfounded premise that Chakma are continuously crossing borders with covert support, poised to trigger a demographic upheaval akin to what some allege occurred in Tripura. However, a critical analysis reveals this to be nothing more than inflammatory propaganda, devoid of evidence and sustained by misinformation.

Far from being a credible threat, this narrative is a textbook example of fear-mongering designed to vilify a community without substantiation. The State Government of Arunachal Pradesh has implemented robust mechanisms to prevent any such illegal influx. Check gates are strategically positioned at various state borders, and additional checkpoints are established along district boundaries to monitor and regulate the movement of non-natives, immigrants, or alleged illegal migrants. These stringent measures ensure that any unauthorized entry is promptly detected and addressed. Official records and data from these checkpoints show no evidence of a sustained or significant influx of Chakma into Arunachal Pradesh, either from neighbouring states or from Bangladesh. The absence of documented proof dismantles the claim of ongoing illegal migration, exposing it as a hollow accusation.

Moreover, the suggestion that Chakma from Mizoram and Tripura are migrating en-masse to Arunachal Pradesh is not only illogical but also contradicts the lived realities of the Chakma communities in those states. In Mizoram, Chakma benefit from the Chakma Autonomous District Council, which grants them significant administrative autonomy and safeguards their tribal rights. Similarly, in Tripura, the Tripura Tribal Areas Autonomous District Council ensures their welfare and representation as a tribal population. Chakma in these states enjoy access to education, healthcare, and economic opportunities without the deprivation or alienation that might drive migration. Their quality of life in Mizoram and Tripura far surpasses what they could expect in Arunachal Pradesh, where they lack comparable political or social standing. The idea that they would abandon these advantages to settle illegally in a less hospitable region defies reason.

The political integration of Chakma in Mizoram and Tripura further undermines this false narrative. In Tripura, prominent figures like Ms. Santona Chakma[58], who serves as Cabinet Minister for Industries & Commerce, Jail (Home), and Welfare of OBCs, and Mr. Sambhulal Chakma, a sitting MLA, exemplify the community's entrenched presence and influence. Likewise, in Mizoram, Mr. Rashik Mohan Chakma and Mrs. Prova Chakma[59] hold positions as MLAs, reflecting the Chakma' active participation in governance. This level of representation stands in stark contrast to Arunachal Pradesh, where Chakma have no such political foothold. Why, then, would a community with established rights, autonomy, and leadership in their home states risk uprooting themselves to face uncertainty and hostility elsewhere? The answer is clear: they would not.

Upon scrutiny, the allegation of ongoing illegal Chakma migration crumbles under the weight of its own inconsistencies. No

---

[58] *Official Portal of Government of Tripura, Council of Ministers,*
https://tripura.gov.in/council-ministers
[59] *Members for 9th Mizoram State Legislative Assembly,*
http://mizoram.nic.in/gov/mla.htm

credible statistics, government reports, or verifiable incidents support the claim. Instead, it appears to be a relic of outdated propaganda, perpetuated by those with vested interests in sowing discord. The State Government's vigilant border management, coupled with the Chakma' stable and prosperous existence in Mizoram and Tripura, renders this narrative implausible. To persist in peddling this myth is to ignore facts in favour of divisive fiction. The Chakma are not a threat to Arunachal Pradesh's demographic fabric; they are a community thriving within their rightful domains, with no incentive or evidence to suggest otherwise. This so-called crisis of illegal migration is, in truth, a manufactured controversy that fails any test of reason or evidence.

4

CONDITIONAL CITIZENS – THE UNIQUE STATUS OF CHAKMA AND HAJONGS

In the preceding chapters, we systematically dismantled the myths, misrepresentations, and misinformation surrounding the Chakma and Hajongs of Arunachal Pradesh. We established, with legal precision and historical clarity, that they are neither refugees nor stateless persons, nor illegal migrants.

Firstly, the Chakma and Hajongs of Arunachal Pradesh do not meet the definition of refugees—either in its classical sense or in the contemporary legal and social context. Their migration was a consequence of historical circumstances, but their status today is fundamentally different from that of a refugee population.

Secondly, while they have been wrongly labelled as "non-citizens," the legal reality is that at least 95% of Chakma and Hajongs in Arunachal Pradesh are recognized as Indian citizens by the law of the land. This legal recognition is not merely theoretical; it is reflected in tangible political rights, such as voting in elections, with nearly 9,300 Chakma and Hajongs already part of the electoral process. However, despite this legal recognition, systemic deprivation of certain rights continues to hinder their full participation as equal citizens.

Thirdly, the persistent allegation that they are illegal migrants is unfounded. Judicial verdicts and official records have time and again affirmed their lawful presence and legal distinction from unauthorized immigrants. This legal clarity removes any ambiguity regarding their right to belong.

Some scholars have attempted to categorize the Chakma and Hajongs of Arunachal Pradesh as **"stateless people,"** [60] a term that fails to hold under scrutiny. According to the United Nations High Commissioner for Refugees (UNHCR), a stateless person is someone who is not recognized as a citizen by any country.[61] This definition clearly does not apply to the Chakma and Hajongs, who, as demonstrated, have legal citizenship, even if their rights remain constrained.

Given this unique situation—wherein Chakma and Hajongs possess legal citizenship yet experience systematic restrictions on their rights as citizens—that a new term becomes necessary. To more accurately define their status, a term comes to the mind is **"Conditional Citizens"**, **"Limited Citizens"** [62] or **"Beleaguered Citizens"**.[63]

These terms encapsulate the paradox of their existence: legally acknowledged as Indian citizens yet subjected to conditions that prevent them from fully exercising their rights.

These terms encapsulate the paradox of their existence: while the law [Section 3(1)(a) Citizenship Act, 1955] recognized them as Indian citizens, they remain subject to conditions that limit their full

---

[60] *Executive Summary of the Report on 'The State of Being Stateless: A Case Study of the Chakma of Arunachal Pradesh' 1. 2025, http://www.mcrg.ac.in/statelessness.pdf*
Deepak K. Singh, Stateless in South Asia: The Chakma between Bangladesh and India (New Delhi: SAGE Publications, 2010) https://www.researchgate.net/publication/360207455_Statelessness_A_Study_of_Chakma_Refugees_of_Arunachal_Pradesh
[61] *United Nations High Commissioner for Refugees (UNHCR), Definition of Stateless Persons, https://www.unhcr.org/ibelong/wp-content/uploads/1954-Convention-relating-to-the-Status-of-Stateless-Persons_ENG.pdf*
[62] *Displaced, And Defiant: The Chakma's Fight for Citizenship, https://www.hinducollegegazette.com/post/displaced-denied-and-defiant-the-chakma-s-fight-for-citizenship-in-a-changing-india*
[63] *https://crdo.chakma.in/faqs-chakma-and-hajong-tribes-of-arunachal-pradesh-2/*

exercise of rights as citizens [64]. However, by no logical reasoning can the Chakma and Hajongs be categorized as Refugees, Non-Citizens, Stateless Persons, or Illegal Migrants.

4.1. THE CONCEPT AND MANIFESTATIONS OF "LIMITED CITIZENSHIP" FOR CHAKMA AND HAJONGS

In the context of the Chakma and Hajongs in Arunachal Pradesh, **"limited citizenship"** refers to a situation where individuals, despite a legal basis for their claim to Indian citizenship and repeated affirmations by the Supreme Court, face significant restrictions and discrimination in the enjoyment of their rights compared to other citizens of India [65]. This manifests in various ways, impacting their access to fundamental rights and opportunities. One prominent example is the denial and subsequent cancellation of Residence Proof Certificates (RPCs) by the Arunachal Pradesh government.[66] These certificates, while not equivalent to citizenship, serve as crucial documents for establishing residency and are often required for accessing various services and opportunities, including government jobs and higher education.[67] The denial of RPCs effectively limits the ability of Chakma and Hajongs to secure government employment,

---

[64] *The Chakma' Struggle for Citizenship: Breaking Down India's Citizenship Acquisition Regime, Moosa Izzat-NUJS Law Review 15 NUJS L. Rev. 3-4 (2022)* https://nujslawreview.org/wp-content/uploads/2023/06/15.3-4.Izzat_.pdf
[65] *Displaced, Denied, And Defiant: The Chakma's Fight for Citizenship,* https://www.hinducollegegazette.com/post/displaced-denied-and-defiant-the-chakma-s-fight-for-citizenship-in-a-changing-india
[66] *Arunachal: Chakma and Hajong Tribes Protest to Get Rid of the 'Refugee'Tag,* https://www.newsclick.in/arunachal-chakma-and-hajong-tribes-protest-get-rid-refugee-tag
[67] *Why Chakma and Hajongs in Arunachal Pradesh are demanding their residence proof papers back,* https://scroll.in/article/1041201/why-Chakma-and-hajongs-in-arunachal-pradesh-are-demanding-their-residence-proof-papers-back

hindering their economic progress and perpetuating their marginalization.[64] Similarly, the lack of residential proof creates significant barriers to accessing higher education, particularly in government-aided institutions outside the state, thereby limiting their future prospects.[64]

Furthermore, there are indications and media report that even if recognized and accepted citizens by the State Government, Chakma and Hajongs in Arunachal Pradesh might not be given full rights to land ownership within the state.[68] This potential differential treatment would place them on an unequal footing compared to other citizens and further restrict their ability to fully integrate into the socio-economic fabric of the state. While some Chakma and Hajongs have been included in electoral rolls, granting them limited political participation rights [69], the overall process has been slow and faced considerable resistance.[62] The extent of their effective political participation and representation might still be limited due to their precarious citizenship status and the prevailing social and political climate. Chakma and Hajongs in Arunachal Pradesh have faced denial of ration cards and exclusion from certain government welfare schemes, impacting their access to essential services and further exacerbating their vulnerability.[70] The constant threat of relocation,

---

[68] *Chakma, Hajong refugees to get Indian citizenship. All you need to know, https://www.indiatoday.in/india/story/chakma-hajong-refugee-indian-citizenship-1043986-2017-09-13*
Open letter: Dear Rajnath Singh, the 'limited citizenship' for Chakma is too little, too late, Mahendra Chakma https://scroll.in/article/851111/open-letter-dear-rajnath-singh-the-limited-citizenship-for-Chakma-is-too-little-too-late
[69] *International Journal of Advance Research, IJOAR .org, Dr. Bindu Ranjan Chakma, https://archive.nyu.edu/bitstream/2451/44215/2/BETWEEN-AGONY-AND-HOPE-THE-CHAKMA-REFUGEES-OF-ARUNACHAL-PRADESH-OF-INDIA%20%281%29.pdf*
[70] *A Question of Citizenship: The Case of the Chakma-Hajong Refugees - SPRF, Arunav Chetia, https://sprf.in/a-question-of-citizenship-the-case-of-the-chakma-hajong-refugees/*

fuelled by statements from political leaders and the demands of local organizations, coupled with the social stigma associated with being labelled "refugees" or "outsiders," can significantly restrict their sense of belonging and freedom of movement within the country.[68] The denial of seemingly basic documents like RPCs has a cascading effect, limiting access to a wide range of fundamental rights and opportunities, effectively demonstrating how "limited citizenship" operates in practice.[64] This situation underscores the interconnectedness of rights and how the denial of one can lead to the infringement of many others, trapping the community in a cycle of marginalization and limited opportunities. The differential treatment experienced by Chakma and Hajongs in Arunachal Pradesh compared to those in other northeastern states, where their citizenship is largely accepted, strongly suggests a deliberate policy of exclusion at the state level, despite national legal provisions and repeated orders from the Supreme Court.[64] This highlights the complexities of federalism in India, where state-level policies and local socio-political dynamics can significantly impact the rights and status of certain communities, even when those rights are legally recognized at the national level.

4.2. CHAKMA AND HAJONGS AS CONDITIONAL OR LIMITED CITIZENS: A CONSTITUTIONAL PARADOX

The Chakma and Hajongs of Arunachal Pradesh, despite being legally recognized as Indian citizens, experience systematic restrictions that limit their ability to fully exercise their constitutional rights. Out of the six **Fundamental Rights** enshrined in **Part III of the Indian Constitution**, Chakma and Hajongs are effectively denied crucial rights, particularly concerning **equality in public employment and participation in governance**. This selective denial of rights creates a paradox in which Chakma andHajongs are legal citizens in principle but face structural barriers in practice, reinforcing the notion that they are **"Conditional Citizens" or "Limited Citizens."**

(a) *The Right to Equality and Equal Opportunity in Public Employment*

One of the fundamental rights most explicitly denied to the Chakma and Hajongs in Arunachal Pradesh is **Article 16 of the Constitution**, which guarantees **equal opportunity in public employment**.[71] In reality, there is no such opportunity for Chakma and Hajongs in government jobs in Arunachal Pradesh. Discriminatory practices and systemic policies ensure that Chakma and Hajongs are either denied government employment outright or face institutionalized barriers that prevent their recruitment into public service. This is a direct violation of the fundamental principle of equality under Article 16, reinforcing their status as **second-class citizens** despite holding Indian citizenship.

(b) *The Right to Vote and Participation in Elections*

The **Right to Vote and Participate in Elections** is a cornerstone of democracy. While Chakma and Hajongs in Arunachal Pradesh are allowed to vote in **Parliamentary and State Assembly elections**, they are systematically excluded from participating in **local body (Panchayati Raj) elections**.[72] This denial effectively disenfranchises them from decision-making processes at the grassroots level, depriving them of political

---

[71] *Article 16 in Constitution of India, Equality of opportunity in matters of public employment, https://indiankanoon.org/doc/211089/*
[72] *The Arunachal Pradesh Panchayati Raj Act,1997, https://secap.nic.in/docs/Act/AP_PR_ACT.pdf*

representation and local governance rights. This selective disenfranchisement further proves that Chakma and Haongs are only **conditionally** accepted within the Indian democratic framework, as their political agency remains restricted.

The Chakma and Hajong communities, recognized as citizens by birth, had approached the judiciary seeking inclusion in the Panchayati Raj system and enrolment in the Panchayat Electoral Roll. This plea was initially presented through PIL-20-2017 before the Gauhati High Court at Itanagar. The case has since progressed to the Supreme Court of India and remains sub-judice under **SLP (C) 14115 of 2022**, titled *Kali Ratan Chakma and Ors Vs State of Arunachal Pradesh and Ors.* [73]

(c) *Exclusion from Welfare Schemes and Socio-Economic Rights*

Various welfare schemes launched by the Government of India, such as **poverty alleviation programs, health insurance schemes, and employment guarantee schemes**, are intended to provide socio-economic security to Indian citizens. These schemes, while **not fundamental rights**, derive their legal authority from the **Directive Principles of State Policy (DPSP)** and various statutory provisions. However, the Chakma of Arunachal Pradesh face **severe gaps in implementation and delivery** of these welfare programs.

(i) *Denial of Legal and Statutory Rights*

Legal entitlements such as the **Right to Food (National Food Security Act, 2013), Right to Work (MGNREGA), and Right to**

---

[73] *The Supreme Court of India, SLP (C) 14115 of 2022, Kali Ratan Chakma and Ors Vs State of Arunachal Pradesh and Ors.*
https://www.sci.gov.in/case-status-case-no/
The Gauhati High Court PIL No. 20 of 2017,
https://hcservices.ecourts.gov.in/

Health (Ayushman Bharat) are either inconsistently applied or outright denied to Chakma and Hajongs. They often face bureaucratic hurdles, discriminatory policies, and administrative neglect that prevent them from accessing these rights, even when they are legally eligible.

(ii) *Exclusion from Socio-Economic Welfare Entitlements*

While **Directive Principles of State Policy (DPSP)** aim to ensure social justice and economic welfare, in practice, these principles are **rarely enforced** in favour of the Chakma. For example, the **Pradhan Mantri Awas Yojana (PMAY)** for housing, **National Rural Livelihood Mission (NRLM)** for self-employment, and **various scholarship schemes for students** are either denied to them or inconsistently applied, leaving them in a state of socio-economic vulnerability.

(iii) *Lack of Access to Government Privileges and Benefits*

Many government privileges such as **financial assistance for start-ups, agriculture subsidies, and social security schemes** are selectively denied to Chakma and Hajongs. Even when they qualify, local administrative bodies often delay or reject their applications, reinforcing systemic exclusion.

Rights and Welfare Entitlements of Chakma and Hajongs: Available vs. Denied

Rights & Entitlements	Available	Denied
Fundamental Rights (Part III of the Constitution)	i) Right to Equality (Articles 14, 15, 17 & 18) ii) Right to Freedom (Articles 19–22) iii) Right Against Exploitation (Articles 23–24) iv) Right to Freedom of Religion (Articles 25–28) v) Cultural and Educational Rights (Articles 29–30) vi) Right to Constitutional Remedies (Article 32)	Right to Equality (Article 16) **Equal opportunity in public employment (Article 16)**
Voting Rights Available to Indian Citizens Only	Right to Vote and Participate in Parliamentary & Legislative Elections	**Right to Vote and Participate in local body elections. (Panchayat)**
Legal and Statutory Rights	i) Right to Education: The Right to Education (RTE) Act, 2009, ensures free and compulsory education for children aged 6–14.	1) **Right to Work:** Under the Mahatma Gandhi National Rural Employment Guarantee Act (MGNREGA), citizens are entitled to 100 days

	ii) Pradhan Mantri Garib Kalyan Yojana (PMGK Anna Yojana) Food Security: Free food grains (5 kg rice/wheat + 1 kg pulses per person per month) for 80 crore beneficiaries under the Public Distribution System (PDS) but available to only Chakma voters.	of wage employment per year. 2) **Right to Food:** Under the National Food Security Act (NFSA), 2013, eligible households are entitled to subsidized food grains. 3) **Right to Health Services:** While not a fundamental right, schemes like Ayushman Bharat (PM-JAY) provide free health insurance for low-income families.
Rights & Entitlements	*Available*	*Denied*
Financial Inclusion & Social Security	Pradhan Mantri Jan Dhan Yojana (PMJDY) for financial inclusion	1) **Atal Pension Yojana (APY)** for old-age income support 2) **Pradhan Mantri Mudra Yojana (PMMY)** – Provides micro-financing options to small businesses and entrepreneurs. 3) **Stand Up India Scheme** – Supports women, SC, and ST

		entrepreneurs by offering bank loans
Poverty Alleviation & Employment Generation		1. **Mahatma Gandhi National Rural Employment Guarantee Act (MGNREGA) –** Guarantees 100 days of wage employment per year to rural households. 2. **National Rural Livelihood Mission (NRLM) (Aajeevika)** – Promotes self-employment and financial independence among rural women and communities. 3. **Pradhan Mantri Awas Yojana (PMAY)** – Provides affordable housing to urban and rural poor 4. **Deen Dayal Antyodaya Yojana (DAY-NULM & NRLM)** – Focuses on urban and rural poverty alleviation through skill development and employment support.

Rights & Entitlements	Available	Denied
Health & Nutrition	1. **Mid-Day Meal Scheme** – Offers free meals to school children to improve nutrition and encourage school attendance. 2. **Integrated Child Development Services (ICDS)** – Focuses on maternal and child nutrition, immunization, and preschool education. 3. **Poshan Abhiyaan** – Aims to reduce malnutrition among women, children, and adolescents. 3. **Janani Suraksha Yojana (JSY)** – Provides cash incentives for institutional deliveries to reduce maternal and infant mortality.	1. **Ayushman Bharat (PM-JAY)** – Provides free health insurance up to ₹5 lakh per family per year for economically weaker sections. 2. Chief Minister Arunachal Arogya Yojana (CMAAY) - Provides free health insurance up to ₹5 lakh per family
Rights & Entitlements	*Available*	*Denied*

Education & Skill Development	1. **Right to Education (RTE) Act, 2009** – Ensures free and compulsory education for children aged 6–14 years. 2. **Samagra Shiksha Abhiyan** – A holistic program integrating school education from pre-primary to senior secondary levels.	1. **Pre-Matric Scholarships Scheme for Minorities** 2. **Post Matric Scholarships Scheme for Minorities** 3. **National Means-cum-Merit Scholarship Scheme (NMMSS)** – Provides financial assistance to meritorious students from economically weaker backgrounds. 4. **Pradhan Mantri Kaushal Vikas Yojana (PMKVY)** – A skill development program offering training in various trades to enhance employability.
Agricultural and Rural Development		1. **Pradhan Mantri Kisan Samman Nidhi (PM-KISAN)** – Provides direct income support of ₹6,000 per year to small and marginal farmers. 2. **Rashtriya Krishi Vikas Yojana (RKVY)** – Supports agricultural development through

		financial aid for modern farming techniques. 3. **Kisan Credit Card (KCC) Scheme** – Provides affordable credit to farmers for agricultural and allied activities.
Rights & Entitlements	*Available*	*Denied*
Women & Child Welfare	1. **Sukanya Samriddhi Yojana (SSY)** – A savings scheme for girl children with tax benefits. 2. **Beti Bachao Beti Padhao (BBBP)** – Encourages girl child education and welfare. 3. **One Stop Centre Scheme** – Provides support to women facing violence (legal aid, medical support, counselling).	
Government Privileges and Welfare Benefits	Subsidies on LPG (Ujjwala Yojana)	

4.3. SYSTEMATIC EXCLUSION FROM STATE-GOVERNMENT SPONSORED SCHEMES

Despite being legal citizens of India, the Chakma and Hajongs of Arunachal Pradesh face conditional and partial access to legal, statutory, and socio-economic welfare entitlements provided by the Central Government. However, when it comes to state-sponsored welfare schemes, they face complete exclusion.

The Government of Arunachal Pradesh has launched various schemes aimed at improving the socio-economic conditions of its people, covering sectors such as welfare, employment, skill development, health, and entrepreneurship. However, these initiatives systematically exclude Chakma and Hajongs, denying them access to crucial state-funded benefits meant for the broader population.

State-Government Schemes[74] from Which Chakma and Hajongs Are Excluded

i. Chief Minister's Shasakt Kisan Yojana (CM-SKY) – Agricultural empowerment scheme

ii. Cluster Nutritional Kitchen Garden Scheme – Nutritional security initiative

iii. Deen Dayal Upadhyaya Swavalamban Yojana – Entrepreneurship and self-employment support

iv. Chief Minister's Yuva Kaushal Yojana – Skill development for youth

v. Skill Development Initiative (SDI) Scheme – Industry-relevant vocational training

---

74 *The Government of Arunachal Pradesh Schemes,* *https://www.myscheme.gov.in/search/state/Arunachal%20Pradesh*

vi.   Chief Minister Arogya Arunachal Yojana – State-sponsored health insurance

vii.   Arunachal Pradesh Entrepreneurship Development Programme – Business support and incubation

viii.   Arunachal Pradesh Seed Fund Scheme – Startup financing initiative

ix.   And many more…

This blanket exclusion from state-sponsored development programs not only discriminates against the Chakma and Hajong communities but also deepens socio-economic inequalities, leaving them without access to crucial opportunities for growth, education, healthcare, and livelihood enhancement.

(a) Use of Local Governance as a Gatekeeping Mechanism

In India, government-sponsored welfare schemes—whether initiated by the Central or State Governments—are often implemented through the Panchayati Raj system. This decentralized governance structure plays a crucial role in identifying beneficiaries, implementing schemes, and disbursing benefits at the grassroots level. However, for the Chakma and Hajongs of Arunachal Pradesh, a systemic denial of their right to vote and participate in Panchayati Raj elections has led to their exclusion from essential welfare programs.

(b) The Panchayati Raj System as the Gateway to Welfare Benefits

Many Central and State Government schemes are designed to uplift marginalized communities by providing financial assistance, skill development, healthcare, and employment opportunities. The selection of beneficiaries for these schemes is often carried out using Panchayati Raj data, which serves as the primary mechanism for:[75]

i. **Identifying eligible households** in need of support.

ii. **Verifying beneficiary criteria** through local governance records.

iii. **Facilitating the implementation** of schemes at the village and district levels.

iv. **Disbursing financial and non-financial benefits** directly to the identified groups.

Since Chakma and Hajongs are barred from voting or contesting elections in the Panchayati Raj system, they are automatically excluded from the very database that determines beneficiary selection. This exclusion has far-reaching consequences, preventing them from accessing vital government assistance.

4.4. SYSTEMATIC EXCLUSION THROUGH DENIAL OF GOVERNMENT-ISSUED DOCUMENTS

Despite multiple Court rulings affirming their citizenship rights, the Chakma and Hajong communities in Arunachal Pradesh continues to face systematic exclusion from fundamental socio-economic entitlements. The denial of essential government-issued documents has severely impacted their ability to access government benefits, employment opportunities, and economic stability.

The Chakma and Hajongs, despite being legal Indian citizens, are routinely denied domicile certificates, voting rights in Panchayati Raj elections, and access to central and state-sponsored welfare schemes.

---

[75] *Panchayati Raj Institutions (PRIs),*
https://www.nextias.com/blog/panchayati-raj-institutions/

This institutionalized discrimination has led to economic marginalization, lack of social mobility, and continued exclusion from mainstream development initiatives.

(a) Denial of Domicile Certificates: A Barrier to Employment & Education

Domicile certificates are a fundamental requirement for accessing government jobs, higher education reservations, and welfare schemes. However, state government authorities systematically refuse to issue these certificates to Chakma residents, rendering them ineligible for Employment in state and central government sectors. [76]

In October 2022, the Government of Arunachal Pradesh took a controversial step by announcing its decision to discontinue the issuance of "Residence Proof Certificates" (RPCs) to members of the Chakma and Hajong communities. Furthermore, the government nullified all previously issued RPCs through Order No. POL/CH-2/2022-23/100, issued by the Political Department. This move has raised serious concerns about the implications for the civil rights and access to government services for these constitutionally recognized citizens.

Without domicile certificates, even highly qualified Chakma and Hajong youths are unable to apply for government jobs or scholarships, forcing them into low-paying, informal sector employment.

(b) Denial of Trade Licenses & Economic Exclusion

---

[76] *Residential Proof Certificate revoked for Chakma and Hajongs, Order No. POL/CH-2/2022-23/100, Govt. of Aruanchal Pradesh, Political Department*

Chakma and Hajong entrepreneurs face bureaucratic hurdles and administrative roadblocks when applying for trade licenses, effectively preventing them from legally setting up businesses. [77] This restriction has severely impacted economic growth within the community, limiting opportunities for self-employment and financial independence.

- Entrepreneurs are unable to register businesses, limiting access to markets and customers

- Lack of trade licenses prevents Chakma and Hajong business owners from availing government subsidies and financial support

- Denial of licenses forces many to operate in the informal sector, making them vulnerable to harassment and exploitation

The exclusion from legal business frameworks further marginalizes the community, trapping them in cycles of economic instability.

(c) Denial of Land Possession Certificates (LPC): Hindering Financial Growth

A Land Possession Certificate (LPC) is a crucial document that establishes legal ownership or tenancy over land. In Arunachal Pradesh, Chakma and Hajongs are routinely denied LPCs, making it impossible for them to access financial services and economic opportunities.

---

[77] *Employment banned for Chakma and Hajongs in Arunachal Pradesh, Order No. Pol-21/81 29 Sep 1980*

- Without an LPC, Chakma and Hajong entrepreneurs cannot register businesses or firms, restricting their ability to operate legally.

- Banks require LPCs as collateral for business loans, preventing Chakma and Hajong entrepreneurs from accessing financial support to expand their ventures.

- Denial of LPCs results in lack of legal security over land, making Chakma and Hajong vulnerable to eviction and land-grabbing.

Without an LPC, Chakma and Hajong families and business owners face insurmountable financial and legal obstacles, limiting their ability to build assets and achieve economic independence.

The systematic denial of essential documents such as domicile certificates, trade licenses, and land possession certificates has led to perpetual socio-economic exclusion of the Chakma and Hajong community in Arunachal Pradesh. These barriers not only violate their fundamental rights but also obstruct their path to self-sufficiency and progress.

Despite legal recognition as Indian citizens, state authorities continue to enforce discriminatory policies, ensuring that Chakma and Hajongs remain excluded from employment, education, economic opportunities, and government welfare.

The Inescapable Conclusion: Chakma and Hajongs as Conditional Citizens, Limited Citizens, Beleaguered Citizens

Given these systematic restrictions, it is evident that Chakma and Hajongs are citizens in name only but not in full exercise of their rights. Their citizenship is conditional, dictated by the discretion of local authorities and political interests rather than constitutional guarantees. Unlike other Indian citizens who enjoy an unrestricted set of rights, Chakma and Hajongs of Arunachal Pradesh live under a regime of limitations where their legal recognition does not translate into full civic, political, or socio-economic participation.

Thus, while the Indian Constitution grants them citizenship, the practical denial of their fundamental rights, electoral participation, and socio-economic entitlements makes them neither fully included nor completely excluded. They exist in a grey zone of **"Conditional Citizenship"** or **"Limited Citizenship,"** where they are acknowledged but never truly accepted as equals within the Indian polity.

5

A TALE OF TWO REALITIES: THE CHAKMA-HAJONGS AND A MILLION MIGRANTS OF THE SAME ERA

Migration from East Pakistan (now Bangladesh) in 1964 was not an isolated movement of the Chakma & Hajongs alone but a larger humanitarian crisis that affected over 8.55 lakh migrants. According to the Estimates Committee (1964-65), Seventy-First Report (Third Lok Sabha), between January 1, 1964, and December 31, 1964, a total of 8,55,996 migrants entered India, who were settled primarily in West Bengal, Assam, Tripura, Meghalaya, and Arunachal Pradesh (then NEFA).[78]

State	Migrants Settled	Percentage
West Bengal	5,78,438	67.58%
Assam	1,62,330	18.96%
Tripura	1,00,340	11.72%
Arunachal	14,888	1.74%
Total	**8,55,996**	**100%**

In addition to Bengali Hindus, a substantial number of non-Muslim tribal communities from the Mymensingh district, notably the Garos and Hajongs, also sought refuge in India, primarily in the Garo Hills region of Assam.[79] Estimates indicate that around 75,000

---

[78] *The Estimates Committee, Seventy-First Report (Third Lok Sabha) 1964-65,*
https://eparlib.nic.in/bitstream/123456789/4940/1/ec_3_82_1965.pdf
[79] *1 Interrogating Victimhood: East Bengali Refugee Narratives of Communal Violence Nilanjana Chatterjee Department of Anthropology - The Swadhinata Trust, https://swadhinata.org.uk/wp-content/uploads/2023/01/chatterjeeEastBengal-Refugee.pdf*

tribal individuals crossed into Assam in early 1964 [80], with approximately 30,000 of them being Hajongs. [81] Official Indian government figures from June 1964 also reported the presence of 47,900 Christian and 20,000 Buddhist refugees among the total registered migrants, indicating that other religious minorities were also part of this exodus.[78] Notably, many of the tribal migrants in Assam were either Christians or followed animistic beliefs.[25]

Among these, **around 14,888 Chakma and Hajongs** consisting of 2899 families [82] were rehabilitated in NEFA (now Arunachal Pradesh) between 1964-69.

However, while their counterparts in West Bengal, Assam, Tripura, and Meghalaya have now been seamlessly assimilated into the socio-political fabric of their respective states, the Chakma and Hajongs in Arunachal Pradesh continue to remain politically disenfranchised, legally questioned, and socially marginalized.

A Comparative Analysis of Rights, Recognition, and Socio-Political Acceptance

5.1. CHAKMA & HAJONGS OF ARUNACHAL PRADESH VS OTHER MIGRANTS OF THE SAME ERA

When comparing the Chakma and Hajongs of Arunachal Pradesh to other migrant groups who arrived in India during the

---

[80] *Jely 18-25, 1964,*
http://web.stanford.edu/group/tomzgroup/pmwiki/uploads/1310-1962-xx-xx-KS-a-JZW.pdf
[81] *Partition of India and Migration from the Mymensing District of Erstwhile East Pakistan: A Study of Hajong Tribe - SAS Publishers,*
https://saspublishers.com/article/918/download/
[82] *P.N. Luthra, Adviser to the Governor of Assam to M.R. Yardi, Additional Secretary, Ministry of Home Affairs, New Delhi, D.O.No.RR.14/69, Shillong, the 10 April, 1969 (National Archives of India)*

same period, a stark contrast in treatment becomes evident. Nearly a million migrants—including Bengali Hindus, Khasis, Garos, Koch, Rajbongshis, Tripuris, Burmans, Hajongs, and various tribal and non-tribal communities—settled across states like West Bengal, Assam, Tripura, and Meghalaya following their migration from East Pakistan in 1964. Over the decades, most of these groups have gained integration, acceptance, and legal recognition in their new home states. In contrast, the Chakma and Hajongs of Arunachal Pradesh, despite arriving under similar historical circumstances, remain trapped in a cycle of exclusion, uncertainty, and marginalization, with their rights as citizens still heavily contested.

(a) Citizenship Recognition over time: The most glaring disparity is in **citizenship recognition**. Across states like West Bengal, Assam, Tripura, and Meghalaya, the migrants have been granted Indian citizenship or recognized as citizens and no longer face ambiguity regarding their legal status. In contrast, the Chakma and Hajongs of Arunachal Pradesh—many of whom are born and brought up in India—still find themselves battling for rights as citizens. The shadow of uncertainty looms large over their existence, as they continue to be questioned and denied the full benefits as citizens despite multiple rulings from the Supreme Court and various assurances by the Government of India.

The legal and policy landscape governing citizenship for individuals who migrated from East Pakistan to India in 1964 is complex and has evolved over time. India's citizenship is primarily governed by the Citizenship Act of 1955, along with various subsequent amendments.[83] Generally, individuals who migrated to India from East Pakistan before January 1, 1966, were eligible for Indian citizenship under the provisions of this Act as it stood at the

---

[83] *Negotiated Identity: A Study of Bangladeshi Migrants in Eastern India,* *https://www.tandfonline.com/doi/full/10.1080/15562948.2024.241642 4?src=*

time.[84] This would encompass the majority of those who migrated during the 1964 exodus.

Although most migrants have not formally acquired citizenship certificates, they have been widely accepted as citizens in states like West Bengal, Tripura, and Meghalaya as the citizenship laws deem them eligible. However, the issue of acceptance has been more contentious in states like Assam and Arunachal Pradesh, where their status has faced greater scrutiny.

The Assam Accord, signed in 1985, introduced specific clauses pertaining to those who entered Assam from East Pakistan (by then Bangladesh) before March 25, 1971.[85] According to this accord, those who entered before January 1, 1966, were to be granted citizenship. The Citizenship Amendment Act (CAA) of 2019 provides a pathway to Indian citizenship for non-Muslim refugees from Pakistan, Bangladesh, and Afghanistan who entered India before December 31, 2014.[78] This act could potentially benefit some of the 1964 migrants who may still lack formal citizenship.

(b) Government Recognition over time: This divergence is further reinforced in the realm of **government recognition**. Migrants in the other states have long since been accepted as part of the state's demographic composition of their respective states. They are treated as locals and accorded the same status as any other citizen. On the other hand, the Chakma and Hajongs in Arunachal Pradesh are still viewed as refugees, outsiders or illegal migrants—terms that are not only misleading but deeply hurtful to a community

---

[84] *Assam Accord - Supreme Court Observer,*
https://www.scobserver.in/cases/assam-sanmilita-mahshangha-union-of-india-assam-accord-case-background/
[85] *BENGALI REFUGEES, HUMAN RIGHTS AND THE ISSUE OF CITIZENSHIP IN EASTERN AND NORTH-EASTERN INDIA - Amazon S3, http://s3-ap-southeast-1.amazonaws.com/ijmer/pdf/volume10/volume10-issue8(3)/12.pdf*

that has contributed significantly to the development of the region over the decades.

(c) Socio-political Integration over time: The socio-political integration of migrants who arrived in India from East Pakistan in 1964 varied significantly across regions, shaped by factors such as language, ethnicity, economic opportunities,[78] and legal recognition. For Bengali Hindu migrants in West Bengal, shared language and cultural practices often eased their assimilation into the social fabric, despite initial economic struggles and occasional stigmatization as "Bangals."[86] The migrant colonies around Kolkata became vital hubs for community building and political mobilization, often aligning with left-wing ideologies, [78] enabling these migrants to establish a foothold in the state's socio-political landscape. Similarly, across states like Assam, Tripura, and Meghalaya, many of these migrants— numbering nearly a million and including diverse groups such as Bengalis, Khasis, Garos, and Tripuris—have achieved integration over time. They actively participate in the democratic process, voting, contesting elections, and holding public office, thus enjoying representation and a voice in the political life of their adopted states.

In stark contrast, the Chakma and Hajongs of Arunachal Pradesh, who arrived under the same historical circumstances, have faced persistent exclusion and marginalization. Despite their eligibility for citizenship under the Citizenship Act of 1955—which granted citizenship to those arriving before January 1, 1966—and subsequent legal affirmations, many Chakma and Hajongs remain caught in a state of uncertainty, with limited access to formal citizenship certificates. This ambiguity has severely restricted their socio-political integration. Unlike their counterparts in other northeastern and eastern states, Chakma and Hajongs in Arunachal

---

86 *Ghotis and Bangals: Decoding a Very Bengali Rivalry,*
https://www.thequint.com/campaigns/bol/ghotis-and-bangals-decoding-a-very-bengali-rivalry

Pradesh are often excluded from local governance structures, such as the Panchayati Raj system. Even those legally recognized as citizens frequently encounter barriers to exercising basic democratic rights, such as voting or contesting elections at the grassroots level, reinforcing their marginalized status and highlighting a profound disparity in the treatment of 1964 migrants across India.

(d) Identity and belonging over time: the issue of **identity and belonging** remains the most painful for the Chakma and Hajongs of Arunachal Pradesh. While other migrant groups of the same era have been able to carve out a space and identity in their respective states, the Chakma and Hajongs in Arunachal Pradesh still struggle to claim their rightful place in a land where they were born, raised, and have contributed immensely. Despite decades of residence, service to the nation, and legal victories, they continue to be denied the emotional and social recognition that forms the bedrock of true citizenship.

(e) Legal and Administrative Treatment over time: The legal and administrative treatment of the Chakma and Hajongs also reflects a troubling bias. Nowhere else in the country are these other migrants still called "illegal settlers" or "refugees." These labels have been discarded in favour of a more inclusive narrative of belonging. But in Arunachal Pradesh, the Chakma and Hajongs continue to be branded as refugees, foreigners, or illegal immigrants—terms that have not only been administratively disproven but also socially weaponized against them.

Conclusion: The migration from East Pakistan to India in 1964, sparked by severe communal violence, stands as a pivotal moment in history, displacing approximately 8.55 lakh individuals. Predominantly Bengali Hindus, this exodus also encompassed significant numbers of tribal groups such as the Garos and Hajongs, alongside other religious minorities. West Bengal, Assam, and Tripura emerged as the primary destinations, with settlement patterns initially shaped by geographical closeness and cultural similarities. The journey toward socio-political integration for these migrants was intricate and uneven, driven by factors like linguistic ties, ethnic identity, and economic prospects. In West Bengal, Bengali Hindus often found a smoother path to integration due to shared language and culture, despite early challenges. However, in the Northeast—particularly for the Chakma and Hajongs in Arunachal Pradesh—the experience was fraught with demographic tensions and inter-community friction, leading to prolonged struggles for acceptance. For the Chakma and Hajongs, social recognition remained elusive, conditional, and slow to develop, as they frequently contended with discrimination and the enduring labels of "refugee" or "illegal migrant."

The legal framework governing the citizenship of these 1964 migrants is a tapestry of complexity, woven from the Citizenship Act of 1955, regional pacts like the Assam Accord, and newer laws such as the Citizenship Amendment Act (CAA) of 2019. Together, these measures have largely resolved citizenship ambiguities in states like Assam and West Bengal, securing full citizenship rights for most migrants. Yet, for the Chakma and Hajongs of Arunachal Pradesh, a striking disparity persists. Despite legal provisions that should affirm their status, their path to rights as citizens and integration remains obstructed, underscoring a profound inequity in how this historical migration has been addressed across India's diverse regions.

5.2. HAJONGS OF ARUNACHAL PRADESH VS HAJONGS MIGRANTS OF THE SAME ERA IN OTHER STATES

(a) The Exodus of 1964: Causes and Context (Hajongs)

The Hajongs, a Hindu tribal group from the Mymensingh District of erstwhile East Pakistan (now Bangladesh), were forced to flee to India in 1964 due to relentless persecution following the partition of India. This exodus, part of a broader displacement of minorities, was driven by communal violence and systemic discrimination against Hindus and tribal communities in East Pakistan. A key trigger was the theft of a religious relic from the Hazratbal shrine in Kashmir in December 1963, which sparked widespread anti-Hindu riots starting in January 1964.[87] These riots, marked by looting, arson, rape, and murder, swept across districts like Mymensingh, Khulna, Dhaka, and Sylhet, targeting Bengali Hindus and tribal groups like the Hajongs and Garos. The East Pakistan government's repressive policies, such as the Disturbed Persons (Rehabilitation) Ordinance, further barred Hindus from selling property, leaving many, including the Hajongs, with no choice but to abandon their homes.[88]

The Hajongs faced additional pressures from economic exploitation, political marginalization, and land seizures, exacerbated by the broader unrest in East Pakistan, including tensions over Urdu imposition and West Pakistani dominance.[89] Alongside approximately 45,000 Garos, around 30,000 Hajongs sought refuge in India, primarily settling in Assam's Garo Hills.[90] The 1964 migration was not an isolated event but a peak in the ongoing displacement of minorities, rooted in the unresolved legacy of partition and persistent hostility toward non-Muslim communities.

Another group of Hajongs who arrived in Assam were initially housed at the Matia Transit Camp in Goalpara district. In 1965, the Government of India's Ministry of Rehabilitation decided to relocate

---

[87] *The Partition of Bengal & Assam - Bounday Report - Documents,* *https://www.partitionmuseum.org/partition-of-india/bengal-assam*
[88] *1964 East Pakistan riots - Wikipedia,* *https://en.wikipedia.org/wiki/1964_East_Pakistan_riots*
[89] *The Independence of Bangladesh in 1971 - The National Archives,* *https://www.nationalarchives.gov.uk/education/resources/the-independence-of-bangladesh-in-1971/*
[90] *Partition of India and Migration from the Mymensing District of Erstwhile East Pakistan: A Study of Hajong Tribe - SAS Publishers,* *accessed April 5, 2025, https://saspublishers.com/article/918/download/*

some of these migrants to the Ledo Transit Camp in Assam, with plans to settle them in the erstwhile North-East Frontier Agency (NEFA), now Arunachal Pradesh.

In July 1965, a resettlement scheme was submitted to the Director General of Resettlement within the Ministry of Rehabilitation, Government of India. The Ministry approved the NEFA Administration's proposal with minor adjustments, as conveyed in their telegram No. F-27(2)/65-RH II dated October 1, 1965. Formal approval for resettling 1,000 Hajong families—new migrant agriculturalists from East Pakistan—was granted on March 7, 1968, under letter No. 27(2)/65-RH II from the Ministry of Labour, Employment, and Rehabilitation. The sanctioned budget included Rs. 17,72,000 initially, later increased to Rs. 38,69,500, for their settlement in the Noa-Dihing Valley of NEFA (under the Pakhan-Deban-Namdapha Scheme).[91]

A total of 504 Hajong families, comprising 2,064 individuals, were transported from the Ledo Transit Camp to the Miao Transit Camp. Of these, 413 families arrived in early December 1965, with the remainder following in February 1966. Upon reaching the Deban-Namdapha area, leaders from the initial group inspected the proposed rehabilitation site but returned to Miao, expressing concerns. Unaccustomed to jhum (shifting) cultivation in hilly terrain, they insisted on lowland areas suitable for wet rice farming. Despite assurances from the NEFA administration and the Ministry's Liaison Officer—highlighting the successful cultivation by Chakma families in similar conditions—the Hajongs resisted. Efforts to persuade them proved futile, and on January 9, 1966, all but 40 families, who chose to remain, voluntarily left NEFA, with the remaining 373 families departing to seek alternatives elsewhere.[80]

---

[91] *Note Sent to the Deputy Secretary (NE), MHA, Govt. of India by R.K. Patir, Commissioner cum Secretary (Home), Govt. of Arunachal Pradesh on 31 May 1980, No. POL-57/79 (National Archives of India)*

(b) Disparities in Rights and Recognition: A Comparative Analysis of the Hajong Community in Arunachal Pradesh, Assam, and Meghalaya

The Hajong community, an ethnic group primarily residing in Northeast India, has experienced divergent trajectories concerning rights, recognition, and socio-political acceptance across different states. A comparative analysis between the Hajongs in Arunachal Pradesh and their counterparts in Assam and Meghalaya reveals significant disparities rooted in historical migration patterns, legal classifications, and socio-political dynamics.

- ### *Legal Recognition and Scheduled Tribe Status*

A pivotal factor influencing the socio-political standing of the Hajong community is their recognition as a Scheduled Tribe (ST). In Meghalaya, the Hajongs are acknowledged as an ST[92] across the state, granting them access to affirmative action benefits aimed at promoting their social and economic development. In Assam, their ST status is confined to specific regions, notably the autonomous districts of Karbi Anglong and North Cachar Hills. [93]

Conversely, in Arunachal Pradesh, the Hajongs, along with the Chakma, have not been accorded ST status. Despite their prolonged residence, many Hajongs in Arunachal Pradesh continue to be labelled as refugees or outsiders, leading to challenges in securing rights as citizens and associated rights. This lack of formal

---

[92] *Tribes of North-East India: A Study on 'Hajongs', GJRA - GLOBAL JOURNAL FOR RESEARCH ANALYSIS Volume : 3 | Issue : 2 | Feb 2014 • ISSN No 2277 - 8160,* https://www.worldwidejournals.com/global-journal-for-research-analysis-GJRA/recent_issues_pdf/2014/February/tribes-of-north-east-india-a-study-on-hajongs_February_2014_1598858860_83.pdf?

[93] *Hajong And Their Bastu Festival, IOSR Journal Of Humanities And Social Science (IOSR-JHSS) Volume 28, Issue 5, Series 2 (May, 2023) 47-50 e-ISSN: 2279-0837, p-ISSN: 2279-0845.* https://www.iosrjournals.org/iosr-jhss/papers/Vol.28-Issue5/Ser-2/H2805024750.pdf

recognition has perpetuated their marginalization within the state's socio-political framework.

- ***Socio-Political Acceptance and Contemporary Challenges***

The absence of ST status and recognition as citizens has rendered the Hajong community in Arunachal Pradesh vulnerable to socio-political exclusion. They often face obstacles in accessing education, employment, and political representation. In contrast, their counterparts in Assam and Meghalaya, bolstered by legal recognition, have integrated more seamlessly into the socio-political fabric, participating actively in local governance and benefiting from state-sponsored development initiatives.

The divergent experiences of the Hajong community across Arunachal Pradesh, Assam, and Meghalaya underscore the profound impact of legal recognition on socio-political integration. While ST status and citizenship have facilitated the assimilation and advancement of Hajongs in Assam and Meghalaya,[94] the absence of such recognition in Arunachal Pradesh has perpetuated cycles of marginalization. Addressing these disparities necessitates a nuanced understanding of historical contexts, empathetic policy interventions, and a commitment to equitable treatment, ensuring that all segments of the Hajong community can fully participate in and contribute to the socio-political landscape of their respective states.

5.3. CHAKMA AND HAJONGS: VICTIMS OF IRONY AND UNAPPLIED LAWS

---

[94] *History of the Hajongs,*
https://thehajongs.blogspot.com/2018/07/history-of-hajongs.html
Explained: The Hajong Tribe of Assam,
https://www.northeastbullet.com/hajong-tribe-of-assam/

The Chakma and Hajongs of Arunachal Pradesh represent a poignant case of historical and administrative irony, where the very laws designed to protect and integrate migrant communities have, due to a twist of fate, left them in a perpetual state of legal limbo. Their story is one of missed opportunities, shifting boundaries, and unapplied legal frameworks that could have secured their future but instead excluded them due to circumstances beyond their control. To understand why the Chakma and Hajongs are victims of this irony, we must trace their journey from rehabilitation to their current predicament, highlighting the key moments that shaped their fate.

(a) The Assam Accord (1985): A Missed Opportunity

The true depth of the Chakma and Hajongs' predicament became evident with the signing of the **Assam Accord in 1985**,[95] a landmark agreement aimed at resolving the contentious issue of migration from East Pakistan into Assam. Under the Accord, migrants who had entered Assam before **March 24, 1971**, were to be regularized and granted citizenship under **Section 6(A)** of the Citizenship Act.[96] This provision offered a lifeline to many migrant communities, providing them with legal recognition and security in India.

For the Chakma and Hajongs, however, this lifeline was out of reach. By 1985, Arunachal Pradesh was no longer part of Assam, having been a separate Union Territory for over a decade. As a result, the Assam Accord's provisions did not extend to the Chakma and Hajongs living in Arunachal Pradesh. Had they remained in

---

[95] *Implementation of Assam Accord Department, Government of Assam, https://assamaccord.assam.gov.in/portlets/the-assam-accord*
[96] *Section 6A, Citizenship Act,1955, Special provisions as to citizenship of persons covered by the Assam Accord. https://www.indiacode.nic.in/show-data?abv=CEN&statehandle=123456789/1362&actid=AC_CEN_5_40_0 0001_195557_1517807319455§ionId=14352§ionno=6A&ordern o=7&orgactid=AC_CEN_5_40_00001_195557_1517807319455*

Assam—or had NEFA not been separated into Arunachal Pradesh as was in 1964 (when Chakma and Hajongs migrated, NEFA was constitutionally part of Assam) [97]—they would have qualified for citizenship under the Accord, given that their arrival in 1964 predated the cutoff date of March 24, 1971. Instead, the administrative boundary shift excluded them from this critical opportunity, leaving them stranded outside the legal framework that could have secured their status.

The Irony of Unapplied Laws

Here lies the crux of the irony: the Chakma and Hajongs were rehabilitated in a region that was part of Assam when they arrived, under a legal framework that promised integration, yet they were left out of subsequent laws that could have fulfilled that promise due to a change in territorial status. The very process of their resettlement—intended to provide them with a stable future—placed them in a region that would later become detached from the legal mechanisms designed to protect migrants like them. If NEFA had remained part of Assam, or if the Assam Accord had been drafted to account for those rehabilitated in areas like NEFA before its separation, the Chakma and Hajongs would not be in this position today.

This irony is compounded by the fact that their exclusion was not due to any fault of their own but rather the unintended consequences of administrative decisions. The laws that could have applied to them—the Assam Accord and the Citizenship Act provisions—remained unapplied in their case, not because they didn't qualify based on timing or intent, but because of a geographical and jurisdictional technicality.

---

[97] *Constitutional History of Arunachal Pradesh,*
https://appsc.gov.in/Index/history

The Broader Implications

The Chakma and Hajongs' situation highlights a broader issue of how historical and administrative changes can inadvertently marginalize vulnerable communities. Rehabilitated with the intention of integration, they now face challenges in Arunachal Pradesh, including resistance from local populations and a lack of clarity about their legal status. Their story is a stark reminder of how the interplay of borders, laws, and timing can create victims out of those who were once promised protection.

The Chakma and Hajongs of Arunachal Pradesh are victims of irony and unapplied laws because their rehabilitation in NEFA, under Assam's jurisdiction in 1964, positioned them to benefit from future legal provisions like the Assam Accord. However, the transformation of NEFA into Arunachal Pradesh in 1971[98] excluded them from those provisions, leaving them in a state of uncertainty. This twist of administrative fate turned a potential pathway to recognition as citizens into an unfulfilled promise, encapsulating the tragic irony of their plight. [99]

(b) The Irony of the Citizenship Amendment Act, 2019 in the Context of the Chakma and Hajongs of Arunachal Pradesh

The Citizenship Amendment Act, 2019 (CAA), enacted by the Indian Parliament, represents a striking paradox when examined through the lens of the Chakma and Hajongs of Arunachal Pradesh. Designed to amend the Citizenship Act of 1955, the CAA offers an accelerated pathway to Indian citizenship for persecuted religious

---

[98] *THE NORTH-EASTERN AREAS (REORGANISATION) ACT, 1971,* *https://www.indiacode.nic.in/bitstream/123456789/1534/1/197181.pdf*
[99] *A Critical Analysis Of State Of Arunachal Pradesh V. Khudiram Chakma (AIR 1994 SC 1461) https://www.ijllr.com/post/a-critical-analysis-of-state-of-arunachal-pradesh-v-khudiram-chakma-air-1994-sc-1461*

minorities—namely Hindus, Sikhs, Buddhists, Jains, Parsis, and Christians—from the Islamic countries of Afghanistan, Bangladesh, and Pakistan, provided they entered India on or before December 31, 2014.[100] However, this legislative measure, hailed by some as a humanitarian gesture, reveals layers of irony and inconsistency when it fails to extend its benefits to the Chakma and Hajongs, the communities of legal migrants in Arunachal Pradesh, while prioritizing illegal migrants from the specified nations.

Understanding the CAA and Its Scope

The CAA's primary objective is to provide refuge and recognition to individuals fleeing religious persecution in their home countries. By fast-tracking citizenship for these select groups, it marks a significant departure from the standard naturalization process, which typically requires a longer residency period. However, the act explicitly excludes certain regions from its purview, including the tribal areas of Assam, Meghalaya, Mizoram, and Tripura under the Sixth Schedule of the Constitution, as well as states like Arunachal Pradesh, Nagaland, and Mizoram, which fall under the "Inner Line" permit system governed by the Bengal Eastern Frontier Regulations of 1873.[101] This geographical exclusion sets the stage for the irony that unfolds in the case of the Aruanchal Pradesh' Chakma and Hajongs.

The Chakma and Hajongs: Legal Migrants in Limbo

The Chakma, an ethnic group primarily adhering to Buddhism, hail from the Chittagong Hill Tracts of Bangladesh. During the

---

[100] *Ministry of Home Affairs, Indian Citizenship Online*
https://indiancitizenshiponline.nic.in/Documents/UserGuide/E-gazette_2019_20122019.pdf
[101] *Citizenship (Amendment) Act, 2019, Applicability of the Amended Act*
https://www.drishtiias.com/to-the-points/Paper2/citizenship-amendment-act-2019

1960s and 1970s, they fled to India to escape religious and ethnic persecution, a plight exacerbated by the construction of the Kaptai Dam, which displaced thousands. The Indian government officially settled many of these refugees in Arunachal Pradesh, granting them legal migrant status with the implicit promise of eventual citizenship. Despite this, the Chakma have faced decades of bureaucratic delays, local opposition, and legal ambiguity regarding their citizenship rights.

In a landmark 2015 ruling, the Supreme Court of India directed the central and Arunachal Pradesh governments to grant citizenship to the Chakma ands and their counterparts, the Hajongs. Yet, implementation has been sluggish, leaving many in a stateless limbo despite their legal standing and judicial backing. This ongoing struggle amplifies the irony of the CAA, which bypasses these legal migrants while extending a lifeline to others.

The Layers of Irony

The juxtaposition of the CAA's provisions with the Chakma and Hajongs' predicament reveals multiple dimensions of irony:

- **Legal vs. Illegal Migrants: A Paradox of Prioritization**: The CAA explicitly targets *illegal migrants* from Afghanistan, Bangladesh, and Pakistan, offering them citizenship based on their religious identity and persecution claims. Meanwhile, the Chakma and Hajongs, recognized as *legal migrants* settled by the government, remain excluded from this expedited process. The irony lies in the fact that a law designed to aid persecuted minorities overlooks a community with a legitimate claim to citizenship, favouring instead those who entered India without authorization.

- **Geographical Exclusion Undermines Intent**

Arunachal Pradesh's status under the Inner Line Permit system renders the CAA inapplicable there. Consequently, Chakma and Hajongs who are classified as legal migrants—they could not benefit from the act's provisions. This exclusion is particularly poignant given that the Chakma, as Buddhists and Hajongs, as Hindus from erstwhile East Pakistan (now Bangladesh), align with the CAA's criteria of persecuted minorities from a specified country. The act's intent to protect such groups is thus undermined by its own regional limitations.

- **Persecution Recognized, Yet Ignored**
  The Chakma and Hajongs' migration was driven by the same kind of religious and ethnic persecution that the CAA seeks to address. As Buddhists in a Muslim-majority region of Bangladesh, they faced discrimination and displacement—conditions mirroring those of the minorities the CAA aims to protect. Yet, while illegal migrants from Bangladesh fitting this profile can gain citizenship under the CAA, the legally migrated Chakma and Hajongs, despite their parallel narrative, are left out due to their legal status and location.

- **Swift Legislation vs. Stagnant Resolution**
  The Indian government demonstrated remarkable alacrity in passing the CAA in 2019 to address the plight of certain refugees. In contrast, the citizenship of the Chakma and Hajongs, backed by a Supreme Court order since 2015, remains unresolved due to political resistance and administrative inertia. This disparity highlights an ironic inconsistency: a new law swiftly opens doors for some, while an existing mandate for others languishes unfulfilled.

- **Missed Opportunity for a Deserving Community**

  For the Chakma and Hajongs, the CAA represents a missed opportunity writ large. Had the act applied to Arunachal Pradesh, it might have offered a resolution for the Chakma and Hajongs who are recognized as legal migrants. Instead, the act's exclusions compound their marginalization, leaving them to watch as others illegal migrants leapfrog to citizenship while their own claims gather dust.

A Broader Reflection

The irony of the CAA in the context of the Chakma and Hajongs is not merely a legal or logistical oversight; it reflects deeper questions about equity and intent in India's citizenship framework. By tying relief to specific religions and regions, the CAA creates a hierarchy of deservingness that privileges some persecuted groups over others. For the Chakma and Hajongs, this translates to a bitter reality: their decades-long wait for recognition is overshadowed by a law that could have been their salvation but instead underscores their exclusion.

In essence, the Citizenship Amendment Act, 2019, embodies a profound paradox for the Chakma and Hajongs of Arunachal Pradesh. It dangles the promise of citizenship before illegal migrants from neighbouring countries while leaving legal migrants—settled, sanctioned, and Supreme Court-endorsed—in a state of perpetual uncertainty. This unapplied law sees its irony "die a thousand deaths" in the hills of Arunachal Pradesh, where the Chakma and Hajongs remain caught in the crosshairs of policy and politics.

5.4. WHY ONLY IN ARUNACHAL PRADESH?

The Chakma and Hajong issue in Arunachal Pradesh poses a perplexing question: why, in the aftermath of the 1964 migration wave from East Pakistan, have these communities been uniquely singled out for political alienation and social marginalization, while millions of other migrants across states like West Bengal, Assam, Tripura, and Meghalaya were seamlessly integrated and granted full citizenship rights? Of the 8.55 lakh migrants rehabilitated by the Indian government, the 14,888 **(out of which only 1798 are alive)** Chakma and Hajongs in Arunachal Pradesh remain an exception, trapped in a state of 'nowhere'. Let us critically examines the roots of this anomaly, dissecting the interplay of political narratives, institutionalized discrimination, and vested interests that perpetuate their exclusion, and proposes a logical path forward.

The Bigger Question: Why Only in Arunachal Pradesh?

(a) Political Narratives and the Fear of Demographic Change

In Arunachal Pradesh, the Chakma and Hajong issue has been framed through a potent political narrative: the fear of demographic change. Unlike other states, where the influx of migrants was managed and normalized over time, Arunachal Pradesh's political and student organizations—most notably the All-Arunachal Pradesh Students' Union (AAPSU)—have cultivated a rhetoric that portrays these communities as existential threats to indigenous identity and culture. This fear, while emotionally compelling, is not grounded in historical facts. The Chakma and Hajongs, numbering fewer than 48,000 (3.5% of the total population of the state as per 2011 census)[102], constitute a tiny fraction of the state's population, and their legal entitlement as Indian citizens—stemming from their rehabilitation by the central government in 1964—is indisputable.

---

[102] *District Census Hanbook Changlang*
https://censusindia.gov.in/nada/index.php/catalog/164/download/306/ DH_2011_1209_PART_A_DCHB_CHANGLANG.pdf

Yet, this narrative has been strategically reinforced over decades, transforming a manageable resettlement into a perpetual crisis.

This stands in stark contrast to states like West Bengal, Assam, Tripura, and Meghalaya, where the state machinery actively facilitated migrant integration. In these states, Bengali Hindus, Khasis, Garos, Tripuris, and other communities—tribal and non-tribal alike—were absorbed into the social and political fabric, often with affirmative measures to ensure their inclusion. Arunachal Pradesh, however, adopted a policy of resistance, driven less by practical concerns and more by a constructed anxiety about losing demographic dominance—a fear that has been weaponized for political mobilization.

(b) Institutionalized Discrimination: A Deliberate Policy of Exclusion

The exclusion of the Chakma and Hajongs is not a passive failure but an active choice, embedded in Arunachal Pradesh's institutional framework. While other states provided migrants with access to land, education, employment, and voting rights, Arunachal Pradesh has systematically denied these communities the same. Chakma and Hajong children face barriers to schooling, adults are excluded from job opportunities, and the community lacks political representation—all hallmarks of a deliberate policy designed to keep them on the margins.

This institutionalized discrimination is reinforced by political rhetoric that dehumanizes the Chakma and Hajongs, labelling them as 'outsiders' despite their decades-long residence. The state's refusal to extend basic rights contrasts sharply with the experience of migrants elsewhere, where integration was not only possible but actively pursued. The question arises: if the Indian government rehabilitated all 8.55 lakh migrants under the same 1964 policy, why does the promise of security, dignity, and rights as citizens not extend to Chakma and Hajongs of Arunachal Pradesh? The answer points to a calculated denial of justice, sustained by those who benefit from the status quo.

(c) A Tale of Two Unions: AASU vs. AAPSU

A critical comparison emerges when examining the anti-foreigner movements in Assam and Arunachal Pradesh. In Assam, the All-Assam Students' Union (AASU) led a fierce campaign against 'outsiders' in the 1970s and 1980s, culminating in the Assam Accord of 1985. This landmark agreement granted citizenship and recognition to pre-1971 migrants, effectively resolving their status and ending the agitation. The Accord demonstrated that a student-led movement could transition from resistance to resolution, balancing local concerns with legal and humanitarian realities.

In Arunachal Pradesh, however, the All-Arunachal Pradesh Students' Union (AAPSU)—which explicitly modelled its campaign on AASU's [103]—has taken a divergent path. Despite the Chakma and Hajongs falling within the same pre-1971 migrant category, AAPSU has not pursued a similar resolution. Instead, it has kept the issue alive, using inflammatory rhetoric to sustain a sense of crisis. Why does AAPSU resist where AASU relented? The answer lies in the utility of the Chakma issue as a tool for political mobilization. By maintaining the Chakma and Hajongs as a perpetual 'other,' AAPSU retains its relevance and influence, rallying indigenous communities around a shared enemy rather than seeking a sustainable solution.

(d) Vested Interests: The Golden Goose of Perpetual Crisis

---

[103] *Kamduk,J.(2016). Rise of Chakma Ethnic Consciousness in Arunachal Pradesh: An Instrumentalist approach. IOSR Journal of Humanities and Social Science (IOSRJHSS).21(5).24-29. www.iosrjournals.org*

The chapter raises a provocative question: do AAPSU and other vested interests in Arunachal Pradesh deliberately avoid resolving the Chakma-Hajong issue because it serves their purposes? The evidence suggests so. Politically, the unresolved crisis provides a rallying point, consolidating support among indigenous groups and deflecting attention from broader governance failures. Economically, the Chakma and Hajongs' status-quo may enable their exploitation as a cheap, disenfranchised labour force, while culturally, their exclusion reinforces the dominance of indigenous elites.

This dynamic is akin to the proverbial goose that lays golden eggs: resolving the issue would mean losing the benefits derived from its perpetuation. AAPSU's insistence on unacceptable conditions—like the relocation of the Chakma and Hajongs outside Arunachal Pradesh—further supports this hypothesis. Such demands are not practical solutions but barriers to resolution, ensuring the issue remains a live wire for political gain. Unlike Assam, where the Accord closed a chapter of conflict, Arunachal Pradesh's leadership appears to thrive on keeping this wound open.

Fundamental and Troubling Questions

The Chakma and Hajong issue prompts a series of unresolved questions that underscore the injustice at play:

- **Why does AAPSU resist a resolution when AASU embraced one?** The contrast suggests intent, not circumstance, drives Arunachal's policy.

- **Why is Arunachal Pradesh the sole outlier among resettlement states?** No other state has denied legal and political recognition to 1964 migrants on this scale.

- **If millions of migrants have secured their place in Indian society, why are fewer Chakma and Hajongs excluded?** Their small numbers make the resistance disproportionate and unjustifiable.

- **If the Indian government rehabilitated all these migrants, why does the promise of rights as citizens falter in Arunachal Pradesh?** The failure lies not in policy but in its execution—or lack thereof.

These questions reveal that the Chakma and Hajongs' unending issue of Arunachal Pradesh is not an accident but a manufactured crisis, sustained by an unwillingness to acknowledge their rightful place as Indian citizens.

RECONTEXUALIZATION OF THE CHAKMA-HAJONG ISSUE

To pursue truth, uphold justice, and foster a genuine understanding of the Chakma-Hajong issue in Arunachal Pradesh, both academia and society must transcend the reductive and oversimplified labels that have long dominated the discourse—terms such as "refugees," "non-citizens," "stateless persons," or "illegal migrants." These descriptors, though entrenched in academic papers, journalistic articles, and policy discussions, serve as little more than intellectual rags, obscuring the rich tapestry of historical, socio-political, and cultural realities that shape the lived experiences of the Chakma and Hajongs. Far from illuminating their plight, these labels distort it, flattening complex identities into convenient stereotypes that fail to grapple with the deeper contexts—colonial legacies (unjustly placing CHT into Pakistan), forced migrations, and systemic exclusion—that define their present circumstances. To truly comprehend the Chakma-Hajong issue, we must peel back these layers of misrepresentation and confront the uncomfortable truths they conceal.

The prevailing narrative surrounding the Chakma and Hajongs of Arunachal Pradesh has been moulded not by dispassionate inquiry but by the twin forces of an emotional majoritarian movement and state-sponsored rhetoric, both of which have cast these communities as perpetual outsiders and refugees. This dominant perspective, steeped in hostility, eschews the rigor of a critical historical or legal framework. Instead, it leans heavily on political grandstanding, cherry-picked facts, and a deliberate construction of "otherness" that positions the Chakma and Hajongs as threats to the cultural and demographic fabric of Arunachal

Pradesh. Such a narrative is not merely incomplete—it is actively exclusionary, sidelining evidence of their deep-rooted ties to the land and their legal standing in favour of a myopic, populist agenda that thrives on division rather than dialogue.

Re-contextualizing the Chakma-Hajong issue is, therefore, not a mere academic indulgence; it is an urgent moral and practical imperative. Justice and equitable policymaking hinge on dismantling the current discourse, which cloaks these communities in terms laden with negativity—outsiders, infiltrators, illegal migrants, burdens—and replacing it with a framework that honours their historical belonging, affirms their legal entitlements, and reflects their socio-political realities. Without this fundamental shift, the Chakma and Hajongs will remain ensnared in a cycle of marginalization, their voices drowned out by an exclusionary narrative that denies them agency, dignity, and their rightful place within the Indian polity. To re-contextualize is to rehumanize—to see beyond the labels and recognize the people they have obscured for far too long.

This book has laid the groundwork for such a reimagining. In Chapter 1, *Beyond the Label: Re-evaluating the Status of the Chakma and Hajongs*, I have demonstrated, through meticulous comparative analysis with groups like the Tibetans and other refugee populations, that the Chakma and Hajongs defy the simplistic "refugee" tag so carelessly affixed to them by scholars and society alike. Their story is not one of transient displacement but of a deeper, more enduring connection to the land they now inhabit—a connection that demands recognition beyond the narrow confines of prevailing stereotypes.

Similarly, in Chapter 2, *The Citizenship Debate – Myths and Realities*, I have systematically dismantled the fallacy that the Chakma and Hajongs of Arunachal Pradesh are non-citizens. The evidence is unequivocal: their citizenship is not a matter of conjecture but a settled legal fact. As established under Section 3(1)(a) of the Citizenship Act, 1955, at least 95% of Chakma and Hajong population in Arunachal Pradesh are Indian citizens by birthright— a status reinforced by judicial precedent and statutory clarity. Yet, this legal truth stands in stark contrast to their lived reality. They are citizens in law but not in practice, trapped in a limbo of "conditional citizenship" or "limited citizenship" by systemic denial of rights. The machinery of the state, entangled with majoritarian sentiment, continues to withhold the full measure of protections and privileges that citizenship promises, rendering their status a hollow shell—a promise unfulfilled.

6.1. FROM ACCEPTANCE TO ALIENATION: THE EVOLUTION OF THE 'REFUGEE', 'OUTSIDER', AND 'ILLEGAL IMMIGRANT' NARRATIVE

The Chakma and Hajongs, two ethnic communities originally displaced from the Chittagong Hill Tracts and Mymensing District due to the communal violence and construction of the Kaptai Dam in present-day Bangladesh, were rehabilitated in Arunachal Pradesh between 1964 and 1969. This marked the beginning of a chapter characterized by acceptance and integration into the socio-economic fabric of the region. However, over time, this narrative of rehabilitation and belonging transformed into one of exclusion, marginalization, and stigmatization, with labels such as "refugees," "outsiders," and "illegal immigrants" becoming attached to these communities. This evolution was not organic but was catalysed by socio-political movements and shifting regional dynamics, particularly from the late 1980s onward. Below, we explore the genesis of this narrative, its implications, and the need to re-contextualize the Chakma-Hajong story.

The Initial Phase of Acceptance (1964–1979)

When the Chakma and Hajongs were first settled in Arunachal Pradesh (then part of the North-East Frontier Agency), there was no pronounced opposition to their presence. For approximately 15 years, from 1964 to 1979, they were treated as equal citizens, enjoying a range of rights and privileges akin to those of the local population.[104] These included:

- **Ration cards** for subsidized food supplies,
- **Trade licenses** to engage in local commerce,
- **Government jobs** in state departments and defense establishments like the Sashastra Seema Bal (SSB) and Assam Rifles,
- **Voting rights** in elections,
- **Gun licenses** and designations such as red coats and red caps for village headmen (Gaon Burahs),
- **Access to education and welfare**, including free school books, uniforms, and lodging in Scheduled Tribe (ST) hostels,
- **Agricultural subsidies and loans**, and
- **Medical facilities** at subsidized rates.

This period reflected the ethos of India's rehabilitation policy, which aimed to integrate displaced communities into the nation's fold. The absence of labels like "refugees" or "illegal immigrants" during this time underscores a story of gradual acceptance and recognition. The Chakma and Hajongs were not seen as threats but as part of the region's diverse social landscape.

---

[104] *CRDO: What were the "at-par rights" enjoyed by the Chakma/Hajogns with other local tribal? https://crdo.chakma.in/faqs-chakma-and-hajong-tribes-of-arunachal-pradesh-2/*

The Turning Point: Rise of the Anti-Foreigner Narrative (Late 1980s)

The late 1980s marked a dramatic shift in the perception of the Chakma and Hajongs, driven largely by the anti-foreigner agitation in neighbouring Assam. Led by the All Assam Students' Union (AASU), this movement sought to expel perceived "outsiders" and "infiltrators" from the region, fuelled by fears of cultural erosion and land encroachment. The agitation's rhetoric and momentum spilled over into Arunachal Pradesh, where the All Arunachal Pradesh Students' Union (AAPSU) adopted a similar stance against the Chakma and Hajongs.

The AAPSU capitalized on this regional unrest to construct a narrative that painted these communities as threats to the land, culture, and identity of Arunachal's indigenous tribes. Terms like "refugees," "outsiders," and "illegal immigrants" were strategically deployed to evoke fear and rally mass support. This rhetoric was not rooted in historical truth—after all, the Chakma and Hajongs had been legally rehabilitated by the Indian government—but was instead a tool to politicize their presence and create an emotive, pan-Arunachal movement. The AAPSU played on a "fear psychosis," alleging that these communities would overwhelm local resources and undermine tribal autonomy, despite their small population and decades of peaceful coexistence.

From Integration to Exclusion: The Systematic Withdrawal of Rights

The AAPSU's agitation had tangible consequences. As Arunachal Pradesh transitioned from a Union Territory to a full-fledged state in 1987, the state government began systematically stripping the Chakma and Hajongs of the rights they had once enjoyed. Ration cards, trade licenses, voting rights, and access to government jobs were revoked one by one, plunging these communities into a state of helplessness. This process of **"de-rehabilitation"** and **"de-Indianization"** contradicted their legal status as Indian citizens—both by birth and through the rehabilitation completed in the 1960s—yet it aligned with the exclusionary narrative that had taken hold.

By the 1990s, the Chakma and Hajongs found themselves in a limbo: neither recognized as citizens with full rights nor provided refugee allowances or protections. Their current status can be described as **"beleaguered Indian citizens"**[104]—a people denied basic opportunities, citizenship rights, and facilities despite their lawful presence in India for over half a century.

The Overlooked Chapter and the Need for Re-Contextualization

The story of the Chakma and Hajongs from 1964 to 1979—a period of acceptance and integration—is often ignored in contemporary discussions, which focus solely on their present marginalization. This omission distorts the historical reality and perpetuates a misleading narrative that casts them as perpetual outsiders. Re-contextualizing their journey by highlighting this initial phase of rehabilitation is essential for understanding the injustice they face today. It reveals how a community once embraced as part of India's pluralistic society was abruptly alienated due to external political influences rather than any inherent conflict with local populations.

The labels of "refugee," "outsider," and "illegal immigrant" are not only rhetorical and misleading but also carry racial and negative connotations that dehumanize the Chakma and Hajongs. These tags emerged not from their actions or status but from a deliberate campaign to exclude them, driven by the anti-foreigner agitation's snowball effect in the late 1980s. Recognizing this historical shift challenges the legitimacy of the current narrative and underscores the need for a more nuanced, truth-based approach to their plight.

The genesis of the "refugee," "outsider," and "illegal immigrant" narrative against the Chakma and Hajongs reflects a transition from acceptance to alienation, orchestrated by socio-political forces rather than organic community tensions. From 1964 to 1979, they were integrated citizens; post-1980s, they became scapegoats of an anti-foreigner agitation that provided legitimacy to these unwanted tags and labels. This period in times -encapsulates this journey, urging a re-examination of their story to address the injustices they endure as beleaguered citizens of India.

6.2. PSYCHOLOGICAL IMPACT OF "REFUGEE" "OUTSIDER" TAGS

The Chakma-Hajong issue in Arunachal Pradesh raises a profound and perplexing question: why, nearly six decades after the 1964 migration wave from East Pakistan (now Bangladesh), do these communities continue to grapple with the enduring weight of the "refugee" label? This term, within the local socio-cultural environment, carries a deeply dehumanizing connotation. It evokes images of individuals or groups who are unwanted, despised, untouchable, and perpetually dependent on the reluctant mercy of the so-called "host" state. Far from being a neutral descriptor, "refugee" in this context is wielded as a tool of condescension, a verbal marker of inferiority that strips away dignity and agency. When such a label is imposed repeatedly—over years, decades, and even generations—the psychological toll on those it targets is profound, pervasive, and deserving of rigorous academic inquiry by researchers, psychologists, and social scientists.

The Chakma and Hajong communities, subjected to systemic social, economic, and political exclusion, have been rendered marginalized and depressed populations. The word "depressed" here is not merely an economic descriptor but a reflection of a deeper emotional and psychological state—one born from the relentless erosion of identity and worth. As a grassroots worker embedded within this reality, I have witnessed firsthand the corrosive effects of this "refugee" tag. It is not just a word; it is a wound reopened daily, a quiet violence inflicted on the psyche of individuals and the collective spirit of Chakma and Hajong people. This name-calling has seeped into the self-esteem, aspirations, thought processes, and visions of students, youth, and adults alike, leaving scars that are as invisible as they are devastating.

Growing up in this environment, I, too, have internalized the negative stereotypes hurled at my community. From a young age, I absorbed the message that we are lesser—unworthy of the respect or opportunities afforded to the dominant tribal groups around us. This internalization breeds low self-esteem, self-doubt, and, at times, a gnawing shame about my own identity. It is an insidious process, one where the oppressed (Chakma and Hajongs) begin to see themselves through the eyes of their oppressors, unconsciously accepting their supposed inferiority as truth. This phenomenon, known as internalized oppression, is a psychological shackle with far-reaching consequences. It dims ambition, stifles potential, and fosters a sense of resignation that can span lifetimes. The Chakma and Hajong youth, for instance, today hesitate to dream beyond the confines of their prescribed "place" in society, their horizons narrowed by the weight of a label they did not choose.

Beyond self-perception, the "refugee" tag carries with it a legacy of trauma and fear that reverberates across generations. For the Chakma and Hajongs, the violence, displacement, and humiliation are not distant memories but living wounds passed down through stories, behaviours, and silences. This generational trauma manifests in myriad ways: a lingering anxiety when navigating public spaces, a hyper-vigilance born from years of scrutiny and rejection, and a pervasive fear of authority figures who hold the power to grant or withhold rights. In everyday interactions, there is an ever-present dread—of ridicule, of punishment, or of being reminded yet again that one has overstepped the invisible boundaries drawn by a society that views them as outsiders. This constant state of alertness erodes mental peace, replacing it with a survival instinct that leaves little room for joy, creativity, or trust.

The psychological impact of the "refugee" label, then, is not a singular event but a cumulative process—a slow drip of degradation that hollows out individuals and communities over time. It fosters a sense of alienation, not just from the dominant society but from one's own potential and worth. For the Chakma and Hajongs, this is compounded by the tangible barriers of exclusion: lack of rights as citizens, limited access to education and employment, and the perpetual uncertainty of their status. The interplay between these external conditions and their internal effects creates a vicious cycle, where material deprivation reinforces psychological despair, and vice versa.

This subject demands more than casual observation—it calls for empathetic, in-depth study. Researchers must explore, how labels like "refugee" become weapons of exclusion, and how communities can heal from the invisible wounds they inflict. For those of us living this reality, the stakes are personal. The "refugee" tag is not just a historical footnote; it is a daily burden we carry in our minds and hearts, a barrier to reclaiming the fullness of our humanity. Until its weight is lifted—through recognition, justice, and a reimagining of belonging—the Chakma and Hajong communities will remain caught in its shadow, yearning for a future where they are seen not as refugees, but as equals.

(a) Internalized Oppression:

When I returned home (Arunachal Pradesh) from Delhi in 2014 and settled back into the rhythm of life among my people, I felt the invisible chains the Chakma and Hajong youths carried. It wasn't a weight you could measure in kilos or see etched into their skin; it was a quiet, suffocating burden lodged deep in their spirits. I saw how decades of being branded "refugees" had seeped into the marrow of our community, especially the young. I saw it in their eyes—eyes that flickered with dreams but dimmed with resignation. I felt it in their words—words that trembled with hope yet crumbled under the weight of a reality they'd been taught to accept.

Since then, I've carried a weight that grows heavier with every interaction I have with the Chakma and Hajong youth and students—a weight born from witnessing the silent, soul-crushing burden of the "refugee" label they've inherited. It's not just a word; it's a shadow that darkens their every step, a whispered lie that tells them they are less than human, less than worthy, less than the dominant tribal communities around them. Over the years, I've seen this internalized oppression seep into their bones, dimming the light in their eyes and shrinking their dreams into fragile, self-imposed cages.

A Glimpse into Their Hopelessness

I've sat across from these young people—students, youths—and listened as they unravel their despair. They don't just feel hopeless; they embody it. It's in the way their shoulders slump when they talk about the future, in the way their voices trail off mid-sentence, as if even speaking their dreams aloud feels futile. They've come to accept that they are somehow inferior, that their place in the world is beneath others—not because they lack ability, but because decades of being branded "refugees" have taught them to see themselves as outsiders in their own home.

I've tried to be a guide for them, offering career guidance and counselling, pouring my heart into words of encouragement. But time and again, I'm met with questions that pierce through my optimism like arrows: ***"What's the point of studying, of working hard, when we have no citizenship, no rights, no jobs? We don't even have a residential certificate to apply for the most basic work. Forget the state government—those doors are bolted shut."*** These aren't mere complaints; they're the raw, unfiltered cries of a generation that yearns to rise but sees only darkness ahead. They want to build lives—for themselves, their families, their community—but the system has convinced them that their efforts are doomed to crumble.

Dreams Reduced to Survival

Then there are those who've stopped fighting the boundaries altogether, the ones who've let resignation settle into their spirits like dust on an abandoned shelf. I've heard them speak with a chilling casualness about their futures: ***"Let me just get a pass certificate for Class 10 or 12. There's no scope for us in government jobs, but maybe I can join the Indian Army, Assam Rifles, or some defence force in the General Duty category—carry a rifle, follow orders. Or maybe Multi-Tasking Staff, sweeping floors, running errands. And if that falls through, I'll head to Tiruppur, Chennai, Bangalore, Gurgaon, Noida—any city where I can vanish into retail, service, or a BPO job,*** [105] ***answering calls for strangers who'll never know my name."*** It breaks my heart to hear them settle for mere survival, to watch them

---

[105] *Chakma Society at the Crossroads: Unravelling Realities of Chakma Youths from Arunachal Pradesh | TICI Journal, Sintu Chakma, http://www.ticijournals.org/chakma-society-at-the-crossroads-unravelling-realities-of-chakma-youths-from-arunachal-pradesh/*

trade ambition for the smallest sliver of stability. These are young people who should be dreaming of shaping the world, not disappearing into it.

The Roots of These Boundaries

But who created these suffocating limitations, these invisible walls that confine their spirits? And how did they come to be so unyielding? The answer lies in a tapestry of history, neglect, and systemic indifference, woven over decades.

- **A History of Displacement:** It began in the 1960s, when the Chakma and Hajong fled persecution in what was then East Pakistan, seeking refuge in India. They arrived with nothing but hope, only to find that refuge came with a catch—a perpetual "refugee" status that left them in limbo, neither fully citizens nor fully free.

- **Systemic Exclusion**: The central and state government promised rehabilitation in true sense but delivered half-measures. Without rights as citizens, they're barred from what that others take for granted—education, employment, a voice in the system. The "refugee" label has become a bureaucratic shackle, locking them out of opportunities and branding them as perpetual outsiders.

- **Internalized Wounds**: Over time, this exclusion turned inward. The constant rejection, the sidelong glances, the whispered assumptions—they've taught these youths to see themselves as the world does: unworthy, unwanted. The oppression isn't just imposed; it's absorbed, carried in their hearts like a quiet poison.

- **A Void of Inspiration**: There are too few role models who've broken through these barriers, too few stories of triumph to light the way. Without proof that escape is possible, the youth struggle to imagine a future beyond the one handed to them.

- **Economic Stranglehold**: Poverty grips their families tight, leaving little room for dreams. Survival demands every rupee, every ounce of energy, leaving no space for the luxury of aspiration.

These boundaries weren't built by the youth themselves, but by a world that forgot them—a world that labelled them "refugees" and then turned away. And yet, the cruellest twist is how these external chains have become internal ones, convincing them that this is all they'll ever be.

A Call to Rewrite Their Story

Still, I refuse to let this be the end of their tale, our tale. Beneath the weight of oppression, I see flickers of resilience—students who cling to their books despite the odds, youths who dare to ask, ***"What if?"*** even as their voices tremble. They are not defined by the labels thrust upon them; they are brilliant, capable, deserving of every chance to soar. My time with them has taught me that the human spirit can endure unimaginable hardship and still yearn for more. And though the road ahead is steep, I hold fast to the belief that their potential is boundless—if only we can help them see it, if only we can tear down the walls that history and neglect have built around their hearts.

(b) How Refugee Tags and Decades of Exclusion Have Scarred the Psyche of the Chakma-Hajong Community

The Chakma and Hajong communities of Arunachal Pradesh carry a burden heavier than the sum of their years in presence in the state—a burden forged by decades of systemic exclusion and the relentless branding as "refugees," "illegal migrants," and "outsiders."

This isn't just a matter of lost opportunities or denied rights; it's a profound assault on their collective psyche, one that has reshaped their identity, their aspirations, and their very sense of belonging. Fuelled by the "go back" chants of the All Arunachal Pradesh Students' Union (AAPSU), amplified by political rhetoric from figures like Union Minister Kiren Rijiju and Chief Minister Pema Khandu, and magnified through the megaphone of social media, this exclusion has reduced these communities to what can only be described as "Depressed communities"—a term historically tied to groups like the Dalits, marked by social ostracism, economic stagnation, political invisibility, and educational deprivation. The toll is visceral, observable in their daily lives, and demands a deeper reckoning.

A Legacy of Fear: Late Movers in Agriculture and Horticulture

Imagine living with an aluminium trunk half-packed, never knowing if tomorrow will uproot you from the land you've tilled. For the Chakma and Hajong, this isn't a metaphor—it was their reality. The degrading labels and the constant threat of relocation have bred a trio of psychological shackles: **fear, hopelessness, and uncertainty**. These aren't abstract emotions; they've dictated the rhythm of their economic life. It wasn't until 1996, when a Supreme Court ruling offered a fleeting promise of stability, that these communities dared to turn toward agriculture and horticulture as a lifeline. Before that, why bother? Why sink roots into soil that might be snatched away?

Even now, the relocation discourse persists, a dark cloud that refuses to lift. When influential voices—ministers, chief ministers, student leaders—casually stoke these fears, the question marks linger: *Will we stay? Will we be forced out?* This isn't just rhetoric; it's a psychological battering ram. The result? A community that hesitates to dream big. Long-term planning—building irrigation systems, investing in better seeds, sending children to school—feels like a gamble when eviction looms as a possibility. They've become late movers, stepping into the agri-horti sector decades behind others, not out of laziness, but because survival demanded caution over ambition.

Yet, there's resilience here. Agriculture and horticulture have become their backbone, a quiet triumph against the odds. But the barriers remain steep: limited access to credit, markets, and modern techniques, all compounded by their "outsider" status. The psyche bears the weight—every harvest is a defiance of despair, but also a reminder of how far they lag, not by choice, but by design.

Shadows of Authority: Anxiety as a Generational Inheritance

If fear shapes their economic life, it's terror that defines their relationship with authority. Decades of harassment, threats, and exclusion have etched **generational trauma** into the Chakma-Hajong psyche, a wound passed down like an heirloom. This isn't subtle—it's in the way a community member's shoulders stiffen at the sight of a khaki-clad security guard or forester. That uniform isn't just cloth; it's a symbol of past abuses, a trigger that flips a switch from calm to hyper-vigilance. I've seen it: the body language shifts, eyes dart, as if they're guilty of existing. Village leaders, too, falter before local officials, their voices muted by the fear of ridicule or retribution, trapped behind invisible boundaries drawn by years of oppression.

This **anxiety and fear of authority** isn't an overreaction—it's a survival instinct honed by experience. The local administration, police, and security forces aren't seen as protectors but as potential oppressors, a perception rooted in a history of evictions, intimidation, and neglect. Trust in institutions erodes when every interaction feels like a roll of the dice—will this be the day they come for us? The psychological toll is staggering: anxiety festers, depression simmers, and a sense of helplessness takes root. Mental health suffers in silence, unaddressed because seeking help means engaging with the very systems they dread.

This fear strangles civic life, too. Organizing cultural events, speaking out, social awareness programme and peaceful protest—these acts of agency feel like luxuries when survival demands staying small and unseen. It took until 2013 for a breakthrough: a rally against drug abuse in Diyun, a cultural event at the circuit house, a peaceful protest in 2014. These weren't just events; they were acts of courage, fragile steps toward reclaiming a voice long suppressed.

Before that, such defiance was unthinkable, the psyche too bruised to risk it.

The "refugee" tag isn't their legal status; but this brand has created a stigma that seeps into every corner of their lives, reinforced by a media that parrots hate and a public discourse that thrives on division. Social media doesn't just amplify this—it weaponizes it, turning every tweet and post into another nail in their psychological coffin.

Beyond Exclusion: A Call for Redemption

The general psyche of the Chakma-Hajong community isn't just impacted—it's been reshaped. They are a people caught in a paradox: resilient yet broken, hopeful yet haunted. Socially, they're outcasts; economically, they're stunted; politically, they're voiceless; educationally, they're left behind. The labels and exclusion have done more than marginalize—they've erased their right to belong, leaving behind a community that mirrors the "Depressed communities" of India's past, burdened by the same traits of despair and disempowerment.

Healing this, demands more than policy tweaks. It requires dismantling the narrative that casts them as perpetual outsiders, a shift in the stories told by politicians, students, and citizens alike. Only then can the Chakma and Hajong shed the weight of these decades, step out of the shadows, and reclaim a psyche unmarred by fear and exclusion. Until that day, their scars remain—a testament to what happens when a nation forgets its own.

6.3. CONCLUSION: REWRITING THE CHAKMA-HAJONG STORY—A TRIUMPH OF TRUTH, HUMANITY, AND JUSTICE

As this book draws to a close, the story of the Chakma and Hajong communities in Arunachal Pradesh emerges not as a footnote in India's complex history, but as a profound testament to the human spirit's endurance against the odds. For too long, these communities have been spellbound in a web of labels—"refugees," "illegal immigrants," "outsiders"—tags that have not only misrepresented their true status but have also inflicted deep psychological wounds, festering under decades of systemic discrimination and exclusion. This narrative, steeped in political expediency and majoritarian bias, has cast them as perpetual strangers in a land they have called home for generations. But this book has sought to unravel that distortion, to dismantle those outdated and unjust labels with the force of reason, historical truth, and moral clarity. Now, as we stand at this juncture, the task before us is clear: to recontextualize the Chakma-Hajong issue entirely, to rewrite their story from a perspective that is organic, untainted by political agendas, and rooted in the unshakable pillars of truth and humanity.

The Urgent Need for Recontextualization

The Chakma and Hajong issue is not a static problem to be solved with superficial policy adjustments; it is a living wound that demands a radical shift in how we perceive and narrate their place in Arunachal Pradesh. The current narrative—shaped by the lens of majoritarianism and the appeasement of the majority by successive state governments—has perpetuated a historical falsehood. It has ignored the undeniable reality that the Chakma and Hajong were not opportunistic intruders but survivors of partition's chaos, displaced from the Chittagong Hill Tracts and resettled in India by the deliberate design of its early leaders. Their presence in Arunachal Pradesh is not an accident; it is a consequence of India's own promise to shelter the persecuted—a promise that has since been buried under layers of political rhetoric.

To recontextualize their story is to strip away these distortions and confront the truth head-on. It is to acknowledge that their exclusion is not a matter of legal ambiguity but a deliberate choice, one that has served the interests of division over unity. This shift in perspective is not merely an intellectual exercise; it is a moral imperative. For as long as the Chakma and Hajong are framed as "outsiders," they remain trapped in a cycle of rejection that erodes their dignity, their agency, and their very sense of self. Healing the psychological scars of this long exile requires more than granting citizenship papers—it demands a societal awakening, a collective effort to unlearn prejudice and embrace a narrative that reflects their rightful place in the tapestry of Arunachal Pradesh.

The Role of Academia in Setting the Right Narrative

This is where academia must rise to its calling. Scholars, researchers, and thinkers are not passive chroniclers of history; they are its custodians, entrusted with the power to shape discourse and influence the conscience of a nation. It is their duty—our duty—to ensure that the Chakma-Hajong story is not hijacked by populist slogans or political convenience. Throughout this book, I have argued with evidence and reason that the labels imposed on these communities are not only outdated but fundamentally flawed. They do not reflect the historical facts of their migration, the legal promises made to them, or the contributions they have made to the region despite relentless adversity. Yet, the narrative has been set against them, calcified by years of unchallenged bias.

Now, the time has come for academia to step into the breach. Researchers must dig into the archives, unearth the forgotten agreements, and amplify the voices of the Chakma and Hajong themselves—voices too often drowned out by those who claim to speak for them. Scholars must challenge the dominant tropes, interrogate the motives behind the exclusionary rhetoric, and construct a counter-narrative grounded in rigorous analysis and unassailable truth. This is not just about correcting the record; it is about justice. By setting the right narrative, academia can help dismantle the psychological burden these communities have carried for generations—the burden of being told they do not belong, of raising children who inherit that rejection as their birthright. Only through such intellectual courage can we begin to heal those wounds and restore a psyche unmarred by fear and exclusion.

A Narrative of Truth and Humanity

The recontextualized Chakma-Hajong story must rest on two bedrock principles: truth and humanity. The truth is stark and undeniable: these are not foreigners encroaching on Indian soil but victims of historical upheaval, woven into the fabric of Arunachal Pradesh by circumstance and resilience. The truth is that they have enriched the state's cultural and economic life, even as they have been denied the basic rights to thrive. The truth is that their marginalization stems not from law or logic but from a politics of division that thrives on scapegoating the vulnerable.

Humanity, meanwhile, compels us to look beyond the cold mechanics of citizenship debates and see the people at the heart of this issue. The Chakma and Hajong are not abstract figures in a policy brief; they are mothers and fathers, students and workers, dreamers and builders. Their hopes—for education, for security, for a future free of stigma—mirror those of every community striving for a better life. To deny them these aspirations is to betray the ideals of compassion and inclusion that India has long professed to uphold. A narrative rooted in humanity rejects the labels that have shackled them and instead celebrates their shared dignity, their unyielding spirit, and their right to belong.

A Call to Collective Action

This book is not the end of the Chakma-Hajong story—it is a clarion call to action. It is a summons to politicians to abandon divisive tactics and embrace policies that honour historical promises. It is a challenge to students to question the narratives they inherit and seek out the truth for themselves. It is an appeal to citizens to reject fear and build bridges of empathy instead. And above all, it is a mandate for academia to lead with boldness, to lend its platforms to the marginalized and its scholarship to the pursuit of justice.

Imagine an Arunachal Pradesh where the Chakma and Hajong are no longer shadows on the periphery but equal partners in progress—a state that draws strength from its diversity rather than division. This is not a utopian fantasy; it is a future within our grasp, forged through dialogue, accountability, and mutual respect. The path is arduous but clear: we must advocate for legal reforms that affirm their citizenship, policies that reflect their contributions, and a cultural shift that welcomes them as kin. Until that day arrives, their scars will stand as a silent rebuke—a testament to what happens when a nation forgets its own.

The Dawn of a New Chapter

The weight of history is heavy, and the journey to heal the Chakma and Hajong will not be swift. Decades of exclusion have left marks that no single book or policy can erase overnight. But the dawn of a new chapter is possible, and it begins with us—here, now. Let this book be the spark that ignites a movement, a reminder that their story is still unfolding, and we are its authors. With academia as our guide, truth as our foundation, and humanity as our compass, we can write an ending that transcends the pain of the past. We can craft a future where the Chakma and Hajong shed the labels that have bound them, step out of the shadows, and claim their place in the light—not as outsiders, but as equals, as citizens, as humans.

Let us wield the pen with purpose. Let us write a conclusion worthy of the justice they deserve, a triumph of the human spirit over the forces of exclusion. The scars of yesterday need not define tomorrow. Together, we can ensure they do not.

EPILOGUE

STRATEGIC POLICY DECISION: REHABILITATION OF CHAKMA AND HAJONGS IN ARUNACHAL PRADESH

In 1962, the Indo-Sino War erupted, shattering Indian Government's illusions of security along its northern borders. The Chinese incursion into Indian territory was swift and decisive, catching the Indian military unprepared and exposing deep flaws in the nation's defence and administrative strategies. One region thrust into the spotlight was the North-East Frontier Agency (NEFA), now known as Arunachal Pradesh. This remote, rugged terrain, nestled against the Himalayas, became a stark symbol of the failure of India's minimal interference—or isolationist—policy.[106]

Before the war, Indian policymakers had adopted a hands-off approach toward NEFA. The idea was to preserve the region's unique tribal cultures and traditional ways of life by limiting external influence and administrative control. This isolationist stance, however, meant that NEFA remained poorly integrated with the rest of India. Roads were scarce, communication lines were weak, and the presence of the Indian state was minimal. While this policy may have been well-intentioned, the Chinese invasion revealed its fatal weakness: an isolated NEFA was a vulnerable NEFA.

The war was a debacle for India. Chinese forces advanced deep into NEFA, raising immediate territorial concerns and humiliating the Indian government on the global stage. The defeat forced a reckoning. Policymakers realized that leaving NEFA detached and underdeveloped had not only failed to protect its people but had also jeopardized national security. The minimal interference policy was abruptly abandoned, replaced by a bold and comprehensive overhaul

---

[106] *NEFA-An Introduction: R.N. Haldipur*

aimed at securing and integrating the region into the fabric of India.[107]

A New Strategic Policy Emerges Post-1962

The Indo-Sino War of 1962 was a stark wake-up call for India, exposing the fragility of its minimal interference policy in the North-East Frontier Agency (NEFA), now Arunachal Pradesh. The Chinese incursion laid bare the region's vulnerabilities—its isolation, sparse population, and lack of infrastructure—and prompted the Indian government to launch a multi-pronged effort to transform NEFA into a fortified and integrated part of the nation.

This strategic overhaul included:

- **Strengthened Administration:** NEFA was shifted from the Ministry of External Affairs to the Ministry of Home Affairs, underscoring its new status as a core domestic priority. The Indian Frontier Administrative Services (IFAS) merged with the Indian Administrative Services (IAS), extending India's bureaucratic reach. New administrative units sprang up, replacing the image of NEFA as a distant outpost with one of active governance.

- **Infrastructure Development:** Roads were carved through rugged mountains, airstrips were built, and communication networks were established. These projects linked NEFA to mainland India, enabling rapid troop and resource movement—a direct response to the military weaknesses revealed in 1962.

- **Economic and Social Integration:** Investments flowed into agriculture, local crafts, schools, and hospitals, aiming

---

[107] *Claude Apri: The Indian Frontier Administrative Service: Romanticism and Hostile Borders,*
https://claudearpi.blogspot.com/2014/12/romanticism-and-hostile-borders.html

to raise living standards and foster national unity among NEFA's residents.

- **Cultural Balance:** While pursuing integration, the government introduced cultural programs and education initiatives to respect NEFA's distinct tribal identity, bridging the gap with the broader Indian state without erasing local traditions.

- **Political Empowerment:** The NEFA Panchayati Raj Regulation was promulgated, empowering tribal communities to participate actively in governance.

This policy shift was a turning point. NEFA ceased to be an isolated frontier and became a vital component of India's territorial and strategic landscape, ensuring it would never again be left undefended or disconnected.

The Population Vacuum: A Critical Strategic Concern

Despite these advances, a significant challenge remained: NEFA's population density was a mere 11 people per square mile. Vast pockets of uninhabited land along the borders with China and Myanmar—akin to a "no-man's land"—posed a glaring strategic disadvantage. This population vacuum left the region exposed to infiltration, territorial disputes, and economic stagnation, undermining the broader goals of the post-1962 policy.[108]

The risks were evident:
- **Infiltration Vulnerability:** Empty borderlands offered easy access for hostile forces.
- **Territorial Threats:** Unpopulated areas could be contested or claimed by neighbouring countries.

---

[108] *White Paper on Chakma and Hajong Refugee Issue, Govt. of Arunachal Pradesh, 1996*

- **Economic Stagnation:** Without settlers, development lagged, leaving NEFA disconnected from India's progress.

Recognizing this, the government concluded that populating these empty zones was essential to secure the region and strengthen its integration with the nation.

Strategic Rehabilitation: Settling the Chakma and Hajongs

In response to these concerns, the Indian government made a bold and strategic decision: rehabilitate the Ex-Servicemen, Mixed Population, Chakma and Hajongs—refugees from East Pakistan (now Bangladesh)—in NEFA's border areas and empty pockets. These communities were offered a new home in Arunachal Pradesh, not merely as an act of humanitarian goodwill but as a deliberate move to address the population vacuum and fortify India's frontier.

The settlement of the Chakma and Hajongs was a cornerstone of this strategy, delivering multiple benefits:

- **Filling the Void:** Their presence transformed desolate borderlands into populated, productive areas, eliminating the no-man's land that had threatened India's security.
- **A Human Shield:** As settlers along the frontier, they served as a living deterrent, making infiltration by hostile neighbours far more difficult.
- **Territorial Assurance:** A settled population reinforced India's claim to the land, reducing the risk of border disputes with China and Myanmar.
- **Economic Boost:** Bringing agricultural expertise, the Chakma and Hajongs spurred regional development, motivating local tribal communities to engage in economic progress.
- **National Unity:** Their integration into NEFA fostered emotional ties between the region and the rest of India, weaving diverse communities into the national fabric.

This rehabilitation was a masterstroke of strategic foresight. Settling the Chakma and Hajongs in Arunachal Pradesh allowed India to transform a vulnerability into a strength, as the borders were now safeguarded by thriving communities. At the same time, it tackled the migration crisis of minorities fleeing communal violence in East Pakistan in 1964. This strategy effectively fulfilled multiple objectives for the government.

The Indo-Sino War of 1962 was a painful lesson, but it catalysed a profound transformation in NEFA. The rehabilitation of the Chakma and Hajongs stood out as a pivotal element of this shift, directly addressing the strategic concern of the population vacuum. Their settlement not only secured Arunachal Pradesh's empty pockets but also laid the groundwork for economic growth and national integration.

This strategic move exemplified India's post-war resolve: NEFA would no longer be a neglected frontier but a vibrant, defended part of the nation. The Chakma and Hajongs, through their settlement, became unwitting architects of India's security, proving that strategic policy could blend humanitarian action with national interest to reshape a region's destiny.

CHRONOLOGY OF EVENTS: REHABILITATING CHAKMA AND HAJONGS IN ARUNACHAL PRADESH

Year	Significant Events/Correspondence
1962	**In 1962, the Indo-Sino War erupted**, shattering India's illusions of security along its northern borders. The Chinese incursion into Indian territory was swift and decisive, catching the Indian military unprepared and exposing deep flaws in the nation's defence and administrative strategies. One region thrust into the spotlight was the North-East Frontier Agency (NEFA), now known as Arunachal Pradesh. This remote, rugged terrain, nestled against the Himalayas, became a stark symbol of the failure of India's minimal interference—or isolationist—policy.
Post-1962	**A New Strategic Policy Emerges:** Post-1962, the Indian government launched a multi-pronged effort to transform NEFA. This policy shift marked a turning point. NEFA was no longer to be an isolated frontier but a vital part of India's territorial and strategic landscape. The Indo-Sino War of 1962, though a painful lesson, catalysed a transformation that reshaped the region's future, ensuring it would never again be left undefended or disconnected.
02.04.1962	**Scheme Proposal to Colonise Vijaynagar and Noa Dihing Valley:** A letter (Reference: A.VIII/1-62/83) was exchanged between the Inspector General of Assam Rifles and the Adviser to the Governor of Assam regarding a plan to colonize Vijaynagar and the Noa Dihing Valley. The proposal, titled "Colonisation of Noa Dihing Valley by Ex-Servicemen of Assam Rifles,"

	highlighted the strategic and economic importance of settling ex-servicemen in the region.[109]
Jan. 1963	The NEFA Development Commissioner made a firm decision to establish a committee tasked with managing the resettlement of families in the Noa-Dihing Valley. The original proposal aimed to settle a varied group, comprising Biharis, ex-servicemen, and former Assam Rifle personnel, in the region, enabling them to make the valley their permanent home.[110]
Feb. 1963	File No. FOR.44/63 (subsequently renumbered as DRS/35/69) provides additional details about this initiative, revealing that the NEFA Development Commissioner had constituted an interdisciplinary committee was formed. This committee included prominent officials like NEFA's Director of Forest (P.B. Kar), Director of Agriculture and Community Development (B.R. Raisinghani), Superintending Engineer (J.C. Chakravarty), Executive Engineer in Margherita (Kulwant Singh), and Base Superintendent in Vijaynagar (L. Mansar), who collaborated to develop a thorough resettlement strategy.
Mar. 1963	Officials from Health Services, the Architect of NEFA Administration, and the Agriculture Department conducted an inspection of the area. Following this, the District Agriculture Officer of Tirap District prepared a

---

[109] *Ministry of Home Affairs, File No. 210(11)/63-NI, "Agricultural Settlement in NEFA: Model Schemes for Settlement and Correspondence Regarding Vijaynagar/Preetnagar Settlements" (National Archives of India).*
[110] *Report of the Committee Formed to Examine Refugee Settlements in Arunachal Pradesh, Established by the Government of Arunachal Pradesh per Memo No. POL.236/72, dated December 8, 1976.*

	comprehensive report, which was later submitted to the NEFA administration.
08.10.1963	R. Yusuf Ali, Deputy Secretary at the Ministry of External Affairs, engaged in correspondence with the Ministry of Food and Agriculture (referenced as U.O. No. 210/11/63/) to seek guidance on the technical feasibility of a **Scheme Proposal to Colonize Vijaynagar and the Noa Dihing Valley**. The objective was to assess whether the proposal satisfied the required technical standards prior to requesting financial approval from the appropriate ministry.[103]
16.10.1963	A report published in The Statesman, written by its Amritsar Correspondent under the headline "Ex-Servicemen to be Settled in NEFA," stated: "The region has ample land suitable for farming. The Central Government is keen to ensure the area is developed to its fullest potential in every way possible.
Late 1963	P.N. Luthra, Adviser to the Governor of Assam and NEFA's chief administrator, held a key meeting with NEFA department heads to discuss settling three groups: (a) ex-servicemen, managed by the Director of Settlement; (b) Assam Rifles personnel, overseen by the Inspector General of Assam Rifles; and (c) landless individuals from nearby Assam districts.
10.12.1963	R. Yusuf Ali, Deputy Secretary at the Ministry of External Affairs, exchanged correspondence with P.N. Luthra, Advisor to the Governor of Assam, regarding the readiness of the **Scheme Proposal to Colonize Vijaynagar and the Noa Dihing Valley**, while seeking the Governor's input as the final authority for NEFA. He noted that, after consultations with relevant officials,

	there was agreement to launch the scheme near the Miao Bordumsa area, in proximity to the road-head.
18.12.1963	R. Yusuf Ali, Deputy Secretary at the Ministry of External Affairs, sent another letter to P.N. Luthra, Advisor to the Governor of Assam, confirming updates to the **Scheme Proposal to Colonize Vijaynagar and the Noa Dihing Valley** following further discussions. They decided to increase the land allocation limit and expand the beneficiary categories to include ex-Army personnel, former NEFA employees, ex-ALC members, and individuals endorsed by the Dibrugarh Intelligence Bureau.
Jan. 1964	The Miao administrative unit was set up, with Mr. Sunil Chowdhury appointed as its Base Superintendent.[111]
Jan. 1964	P.B. Kar, NEFA's Director of Forests, was appointed as the Ex-officio Settlement Officer to supervise the execution of the Miao-Vijaynagar Settlement Scheme.
Jan. 1964	In January 1964, the first wave of migration brought landless settlers, mainly from the Deori and Ahom communities, to the Miao region. They settled in M'Pen, a once-established but now-abandoned village. The Divisional Forest Officer of Changlang Forest Division was given clear instructions by the Director of Forests about the M'Pen settlement plan.

---

[111] *Press India Bureau, Weekly Digest of News, Vol.IX. No. 15 dated April 11, 1965*

20.01.1964	P.B. Kar, NEFA's Director of Forests, was appointed as the Ex-officio Settlement Officer to supervise the execution of the Miao-Vijaynagar Settlement Scheme.
22.01.1964	The Ministry of External Affairs conveyed the Government of India's approval of the scheme for an air-maintained settlement in Vijay Nagar through letter No. 210(11)/63-NI, directed to the Adviser to the Governor of Assam.
22.01.1964	W.S. Rynjah, Secretary (General Administration) of NEFA, issued correspondence (No. For 44/63) to all Political Officers, Department Heads, and Deputy Directors of Supply & Transport in NEFA. This communication transmitted an approved plan for resettling agrarian communities in the Miao-Vijoynagar Area, located within the Tirap Frontier Division of NEFA.
24.01.1964	The Director of Forests in NEFA greenlit an agricultural community settlement plan for the Vijaynagar area, which was also evaluated and supported by the Inspector General of Assam Rifles (IGAR).
25.01.1964	W.S. Rynjah, Secretary (General Administration) of NEFA, wrote to R. Yusuf Ali, Deputy Secretary at the Ministry of External Affairs (No. FOR.44/64,1226). The letter explained that, although the ex-servicemen resettlement scheme in NEFA had yet to be implemented, a simpler alternative plan was being launched. This new initiative focused on resettling a varied agricultural community on unoccupied land adjacent to the region. Essentially, it involved providing

	homesteads and farmland to 200 families in Vijaynagar and 1,000 families in Miao.
08.02.1964	**Migration Crisis**: A national emergency arose with the sudden influx of migrants from East Pakistan beginning in January 1964. In response, a "Conference on the Rehabilitation of Migrants" was convened in New Delhi on February 8, 1964, attended by several Indian Cabinet ministers, select Chief Ministers, and NEFA administrators. The central government urged state governments to share the national responsibility of rehabilitating the migrants by providing vacant land for resettlement. Accordingly, the NEFA administration initially offered 3,000 acres of land to accommodate around 1,000 families.
13.02.1964	The Secretary of Planning & Development, NEFA, directed Mr. P.B. Kar, the Settlement Officer, to screen a long list of Garo, Koch, Barman, and Hajong families— then living in various camps across Assam and the Garo Hills (now Meghalaya)—for possible rehabilitation in the Miao-Vijaynagar area.
16.03.1964	An extract from D.O. No. F-3/64 dated March 16, 1964, from the Governor of Assam to the President of India confirms that the NEFA administration sanctioned Rs. 15 lakhs for settling about 1,000 families—including ex-servicemen, ex-Assam Rifles personnel, ex-NEFA employees, and landless persons from adjoining Assam— in the Tirap Frontier Division. It also highlights NEFA's efforts to allocate land for tribal refugees recently displaced from East Pakistan into the Garo Hills.
19.03.1964	A high-level meeting between the NEFA administration and the Ministry of Rehabilitation

	discussed the resettlement of displaced persons from East Pakistan in the Tirap Frontier Division. Key officials from both sides, including P.N. Luthra, L.B. Thanga, P.B. Kar, and J.C. Chakraborty from NEFA, and Bhagwant Singh, N.V. Venkataraman, and K.B. Mathur from the Ministry, participated. The meeting concluded with a decision to rehabilitate 1,000 families in the Miao-Vijaynagar area of the Noa-Dihing valley.
20.03.1964	On March 20, 1964, a meeting of senior NEFA officials—including P.N. Luthra, R.M. Agarwal, P.B. Kar, P.N. Nag, and L.B. Thanga—appointed P.B. Kar as the Ex-officio Resettlement Officer to oversee the execution of the settlement scheme. A dedicated staff was to be placed under his charge for its implementation.
10.04.1964	The Governor of Assam, Mr. Vishnu Sahay, in letter No. GA-71/64 to Chief Minister B.P. Chaliha, recommended the resettlement of displaced Chakma from East Pakistan—then sheltering in the Mizo District of Assam—in the Tirap Division of NEFA, noting the availability of ample unoccupied land in the
11.04.1964	A note was issued to the Director of Forests (Resettlement Officer), recommending that an allotment of 5 acres per family would be sufficient for refugee resettlement.
16.04.1964	The Chief Minister B.P. Chaliha and Governor Vishnu Sahay of Assam discussed ways to ease the rehabilitation burden of East Pakistan refugees in Assam. The Government of Assam urged the NEFA administration to accommodate 12,000 migrant families in the vacant areas of NEFA.

27.04.1964	In a follow-up to the Governor's April 10, 1964 letter, Assam's Chief Secretary A.N. Kidwai, on April 27, 1964 (letter No. RHM-24/64/10), requested P.N. Luthra, Adviser to the Governor, to arrange for the rehabilitation of 10,000 displaced persons from East Pakistan in NEFA's Tirap Division.
06.05.1964	Referring to the April 16, 1964 discussion between the Governor and Chief Minister, P.N. Luthra, Adviser to the Governor, informed Chief Secretary A.N. Kidwai on May 6, 1964, that NEFA could not accommodate 12,000 migrant families, but could rehabilitate up to 3,000 Chakma families from Assam's Mizo District in the available area of Tirap Division.
July 1964	The first group of 488 Chakma (52 families) arrived in Namphai, Miao, after being screened and registered as refugees in Karimganj (Cachar), and Nowgong (now Nagaon) in Assam.
06.08.1964	In letter D.O. No. GA-195/64, Governor Vishnu Sahay suggested to Rehabilitation Minister Mahavir Tyagi that the 1,000 families to be resettled in the Miao-Vijaynagar valley of NEFA be distributed among the Chakma, Garos, and plains tribal communities from Assam.
12.08.1964	Sunil Chaudhury, Base Superintendent in Miao, sent letter No. STL/62/2/26 to the Director of Forest, NEFA, Shillong, listing 490 Chakma migrants from the first group who had recently settled in Namphai via Tripura.
24.08.1964	Mr. Sahay informed that the Chief Minister of Assam preferred to proceed with resettling 1,000 Chakma

	families as planned, since they were already near NEFA. He clarified this wouldn't conflict with the mixed population policy, as additional resettlement of other communities was also being planned for the area.[112]
25.09.1964	Home Minister G.L. Nanda, in D.O. No. 15/12/64-SR(R)-A to Assam Chief Minister B.P. Chaliha, reported that by August 31, around 80,000 Garos, Hajongs, and Dolus (mostly Christians) and 15,000 Chakma (mostly Buddhists) had migrated to Assam following communal violence in East Pakistan. While tribal resettlement faced little resistance, there were signs of opposition to rehabilitating Bengali Hindus.
10.10.1964	P.N. Luthra, Adviser to the Governor of Assam, noted in File No. PCT-71/63 that resettlement of up to 1,000 Chakma families in the Miao area should proceed. The directive was forwarded by S.D. Lahakar, Deputy Secretary, Planning & Development, NEFA, on October 17, 1964, marking the start of the Chakma settlement scheme in Arunachal Pradesh.[113]
11.04.1965	A Press Information Bureau report dated April 11, 1965, noted intensified development in NEFA and proposed settling around 7,000 East Pakistan Chakma refugees in the Miao-Vijaynagar area of Tirap. By then, 488 had already arrived and resettlement was in progress.[114]

---

[112] *Rehabilitation of refugees and others in Assam including hill districts and North East Frontier Agency. MHA File No. 15/12/64-SR/R-A (National Archives of India)*
[113] *White Paper on Chakma and Hajong Refugee Issue, Govt. of Arunachal Pradesh, 1996*
[114]
https://archive.pib.gov.in/archive/ArchiveSecondPhase/EXTERNAL%20

21.04.1965	With 1,122 Chakma families already settled in Miao, the NEFA administration anticipated more refugees amid ongoing migrations from East Pakistan and Burma. On April 21, 1965 (Ref. No. RR 17/64), Adviser P.N. Luthra requested Political Officers in NEFA to submit detailed proposals on land available for resettlement, including location, capacity, and irrigation potential.
15.06.1965	In a Tour Note dated June 15, 1965, L.J. Johnson, Additional Secretary, Ministry of Rehabilitation, reported that 1,000 more Chakma families were to be relocated to the Miao-Noa-Dihing area and another 1,000 to the Lohit Frontier Division. Discussions with P.B. Kar, Director of Forests, revealed limited land availability near Vijaynagar, requiring 3–4 acres per year per family to maintain a 5–6 year jhum cycle. The NEFA administration was exploring additional resettlement areas, though success was uncertain.
15.06.1965	The settlement committee submitted a tentative report dividing land into nine segments, estimating space for 1,500 more families in the Noa-Dihing valley. Based on family size, 5 acres of WRC or 20 acres of Jhum land were deemed sufficient. The plan proposed settling 500 families in WRC areas and 1,000 in Jhum areas.
22.06.1965	A key meeting at Raj Bhavan, Shillong, led by Union Rehabilitation Minister Mahavir Tyagi and Assam officials, resulted in the NEFA Administration agreeing

	to resettle 2,000 additional Chakma families, raising the total to 3,000 for the Miao region.[115]
19.07.1965	In a July 19, 1965 tour note, H.S. Butalia, Liaison Officer, Ministry of Rehabilitation, reported that the Adviser to the Governor of Assam had proposed resettling 400–500 Chakma families in the Yangsang Tso valley near Tuting, in the Siang Frontier Division of NEFA, along the Indo-Tibetan border.[116]
03.09.1965	In D.O. No. RR.65/65 dated September 3, 1965, P.N. Luthra informed A.D. Pandey, Joint Secretary, MHA, about the civilian resettlement in NEFA, modelled on the ex-servicemen scheme, and included detailed figures and locations.[117]
10.04.1969	In a D.O. letter, P.N. Luthra, Adviser to the Governor of Assam, informed M.R. Yardi, Additional Secretary, Ministry of Home Affairs, that the final batch of 207 Chakma families from East Pakistan had been resettled in the Deban-Namdapha region, completing the relocation of 2,899 families to NEFA. He added that no further intake would occur, noting that the NEFA Administration had earlier agreed to accommodate around 3,000 families.[118]

---

[115] *Record of discussion held on June 22, 1965, between the Union Rehabilitation Minister and senior Assam officials, including the Rehabilitation Minister, Chief Secretary, and other state officers. (Assam Archives File)*

[116] *Tour Note of H.S Butalia, Liaison Officer, Ministry of Rehabilitation, Govt. of India vide No. 13(23)/65-RH. I dated 19th July, 1965 regarding his visit to Goalpara and Garo Hills District and Tripura (Assam Archives File)*

[117] *Development & Resettlement of of ex-services Sectors of the Indo Pakistan border and NEFA (217/16/65-NEFA) National Archives of India*

[118] *Letter of Mr. P.N. Luthra, Adviser to the Governor of Assam vide No. D.O.R.R.14/69 dated 10th April 1969 to M.R. Yardi, Additional Secretary, Ministry of Home Affairs, New Delhi*

Conclusion: A Strategic Legacy Unveiled

The rehabilitation and settlement of the Chakma and Hajongs in the North-East Frontier Agency (NEFA), now Arunachal Pradesh, represent a defining moment in India's post-independence history, intricately tied to the strategic imperatives that emerged in the wake of the 1962 Indo-Sino war. The chronological records accessed from various government archives illuminate the genesis of this initiative, revealing it as a meticulously planned response to both humanitarian needs and national security concerns. Far from being a haphazard resettlement, this effort was a deliberate and coordinated endeavour between the Government of India, NEFA authorities, and other administrative divisions, aimed at transforming a vulnerable frontier into a fortified buffer zone.

Strategic Foundations Post-1962

The 1962 Indo-Sino war exposed critical weaknesses along India's northeastern borders, where rugged terrain and sparse population left the region susceptible to external threats. In this context, the Chakma and Hajongs—displaced from the Chittagong Hill Tracts due to the Kaptai Dam project and communal unrest— emerged as more than mere refugees. Their settlement in NEFA was envisioned as a strategic countermeasure, a means to populate and stabilize an area critical to India's territorial integrity. The government recognized their agrarian expertise and resilience as assets, capable of fostering economic self-sufficiency while anchoring India's presence in a geopolitically sensitive zone.

Administrative Coordination and Intent

The records underscore the remarkable synergy that underpinned this initiative. The Government of India, in collaboration with NEFA authorities and various divisions, executed a plan that balanced immediate relief with long-term objectives. A pivotal document, the letter from P.N. Luthra, Advisor to the Governor of

Assam, dated April 21, 1965 (Memo No 17/64), addressed to all Political Officers and Additional Political Officers of NEFA, articulates this dual purpose with clarity. Luthra's correspondence highlights the settlement's aim: to provide refuge to the Chakma, Hajongs, and other mixed communities while simultaneously reinforcing India's frontier defences in the aftermath of the war. This strategic intent is further corroborated by the Estimates Committee's Seventy-First Report (Third Lok Sabha) 1964-65, which emphasizes the settlement's role in enhancing border security and regional development.

Dispelling Myths and Misinformation

These government records, though only a fraction of the vast archival material still inaccessible, serve as a powerful rebuttal to the myths, misgivings, and misunderstandings that have long surrounded the Chakma and Hajong issue. For decades, narratives of "illegal migration" or "demographic disruption" have distorted their story, often fuelled by propaganda and misleading accounts. Yet, the accessed documents dismantle such claims, presenting the settlement as a state-sanctioned project rooted in strategic necessity and administrative foresight. They restore historical accuracy, affirming that the presence of these communities in NEFA was neither accidental nor unauthorized but a calculated step in nation-building.

The Human and Geopolitical Legacy

Beyond its strategic dimensions, the settlement carries a profound human narrative. For the Chakma and Hajongs, NEFA offered sanctuary from displacement and persecution, yet it also placed them at the heart of a complex geopolitical landscape. Their integration into the region was not without friction, as local tensions and political debates later emerged. Nevertheless, their contribution to the socio-economic fabric of Arunachal Pradesh endures, a testament to their resilience and adaptability.

Geopolitically, the settlement bolstered India's northeastern frontier at a time of heightened vulnerability, signalling a proactive stance in the face of regional instability. It subtly reshaped India's relations with neighbouring countries, particularly in the context of border management, by establishing a living barrier against potential incursions. The initiative's legacy reverberates in contemporary debates on refugee policy and national security, offering lessons in balancing humanitarian obligations with strategic priorities.

Conclusion: Resilience and Realpolitik

In the final reckoning, the rehabilitation and settlement of the Chakma and Hajongs in NEFA encapsulate a rare convergence of humanitarianism and realpolitik. What began as a response to the 1962 war evolved into a bold experiment in statecraft—one that addressed an immediate crisis while laying the groundwork for long-term stability. The unearthed records not only vindicate the government's actions but also elevate the Chakma and Hajongs from footnotes of history to agents of India's frontier resilience. As India navigates modern challenges of border security and refugee resettlement, this chapter stands as a reminder that strategic vision, executed with administrative unity, can transform adversity into enduring strength. The story of the Chakma and Hajongs is not merely one of survival but of unintended yet invaluable nation-building, etched into the annals of India's northeastern legacy.

Annexure-I: Affidavit filed by Ministry of Home Affairs, Govt. of India (Central Govt. is of the view that persons settled in Arunachal Pradesh after their migration in 1964 but before the 1986 amendment to the Citizenship Act would be citizens of India) Page-1

IN THE HIGH COURT OF DELHI AT NEW DELHI

(CIVIL EXTRAORDINARY WRIT JURISDICTION)

CIVIL WRIT PETITION NO.886 OF 2000

IN THE MATTER OF:

People's Union for Civil Liberties & Anr.　　　　....Petitioners

Versus

Election Commission of India & Ors.　　　　...Respondents

SUPPLEMENTARY AFFIDAVIT ON BEHALF OF RESPONDENT NO.3

I, Ajai Srivastava, Deputy Secretary, S/o Sri N. Lal, resident of A-84, Pandara Road, New Delhi do hereby solemnly declare as under:

1.　　That I am working as Deputy Secretary in the Ministry of Home Affairs. I am acquainted with the facts and circumstances of the present case and am competent and authorised to swear this affidavit.

That the answering respondent by way of this supplementary affidavit submits that according to Section 3 of the Citizenship Act 1955 every person born in India-

(a)　on or after the 26th day of January 1950, but before the commencement of Citizenship (Amendment) Act, 1986:

contd..2/-

168

Annexure-I: Affidavit filed by Ministry of Home Affairs, Govt. of India (Central Govt. is of the view that persons settled in Arunachal Pradesh after their migration in 1964 but before the 1986 amendment to the Citizenship Act would be citizens of India) Page-2

(b)   on or after such commencement and either of whose
        parents is a citizen of India at the time of his
        birth
        shall be a citizen of India by birth.

        Accordingly, Central Government is of the view
        that persons settled in Arunachal Pradesh after
        their migration in 1964 but before the 1986
        amendment to the Citizenship Act would be
        citizens of India.

DEPONENT

VERIFICATION:

        Verified at New Delhi on this the
August, 2000 that the contents of this affidavit are true
to my knowledge derived and believed to be correct on the
basis of information. No part of it is false and nothing
material has been concealed therefrom.

DEPONENT
(AJAI SRIVASTAVA)
Deputy Secretary

GOVERNMENT OF INDIA
NORTH EAST FRONTIER AGENCY

No. RR. 17/64   Dated Shillong, the 21st April, 1965

To

All Political Officers/Additional Political Officers, NEFA

Sub :   Resettlement of People in NEFA.

Sir,

Back ground.   The area of NEFA is comparatively thinly populated. For an area of about 33,000 sq. miles, the total population is about 3,37,000. The density of population varies from 4% per sq. mile in Lohit Frontier Division to 21.8% in the Tirap Frontier Division .

Problem of refugees etc.   2.   There has been no land settlement system in NEFA so far, as in the other settled areas and no cadastral survey has yet been carried out. The ownership of land in NEFA varies from tribe to tribe through generally speaking land is either owned by individuals or by the clan. Reports show that there are certain areas with vacant land on which there is no direct individuals or claim ownership.

3.   The country as a whole is facing problems of land for settlement of people on account of the large influx of refugees from Pakistan and Burma. Repatriation of more Indians from foreign countries such as Ceylon and Africa is likely for whom land has to be found in our country. There had also been influx of Tibetan refugees in the recent past. Further, there is the problem of settlement of some ex-servicemen and ex-Assam Rifles personnel, who have no land of their own where they can settle after they have played their role in the defence of the country and retired. All the State Governments are trying to do their best to accommodate the refugees etc. It is desirable for NEFA people also to render help just as other States are assisting.

Undesirability of keeping vacant land in border areas.   4.   The settlement of people in NEFA will also help in developing the pockets that are lying unused and unoccupied by the local population. Besides, the presence of stretches of vacant land along the border is strategically not desirable and the last emergency had high lighted this problem. Resettlement of people in the vacant border areas will help to strengthen our frontiers and their defence.

69

Safe-Guard against undue publicity.

5. The important thing to note, however, is that the people's suspicion should not be roused unnecessarily in bringing people from outside NEFA for settlement. It is also not necessary to publicise widely any scheme of settling people in NEFA. Much will depend upon the approach of the Political Officers. For example, for resettling Tibetan refugees, land was made available by the people when it was explained to them that the country as a whole was in difficulty and that NEFA people should help in the matter. The major factors necessitating the resettlement of people in NEFA are :

    (a)   To strengthen border defence by populating vacant land.

    (b)   To find land for the refugees and Indians returing from foreign countries who have posed a problem on a national scale.

    (c)   Our duty towards ex-sevicemen and ex-Assam Rifles who are engaged in the defence of our country in the present emergency.

6. While progressing any settlement schemes the following important points may kindly be borne in mind :-

    (a)   Land should be voluntarily given by the people to whom an emotional approach has to be made. Such approach should be made by the Political Officer himself and he should consult the leaders in the areas to ensure that our resettlement proposal does not lead to misplaced agitation or misunder standings.

    (b)   Land should as per as possible not belong to any one and this point should be fully cleared herein its utilisation for settlement. There are areas where full rights are not likely to be affected by settlement of people in NEFA.

    (c)   Land may be given to the settlers on lease for which term has tobe prescribed along with the proformas to be singed by the settlers.

    (d)   Where land is given by the people voluntarily there ought to be written agreement about it on either side.

    (e)   Wherever any compensation is needed, it should be duly paid to the villagers and necessary documents prepared.

    (f)   Only that much of land which may be adequate to consolidate an economic holding should be allotted to each family coming from outside NEFA. As a rule, the ceiling for allotment of land to each family of settler should be put up to this Administration for approval.

    (g)   The ground survey must precede any attempts at settlement.

7.   Bearing in view the above points, the Political Officers are requested to send concrete proposals showing the land available in their areas for settlement. The proposal should specify the location of land, the number of families which can be settled having regard to the cultiviability of the area and availability of water for irrigation.

8.   Receipt of this letter may kindly be acknowledged.

Yours faithfully,

Sd/-
(P. N. Luthra)
Adviser to the Governor of Assam.

Memo No. RR. 17/64   Dated Shillong, the
21st April, 1965.

Copy to :-

(1)   Director of Agriculture and Community Development, NEFA, Shillong.

(2)   Deputy Secretary (Political). NEFA. Shillong .

(3)   Director of Forests, NEFA, Shillong.

Sd/-
(P. N. Luthra)
Adviser to the Governor of Assam.

Name of District ...... *Lohit*

Sub-division ...*Namsai*... Circle ...*R.K.m*...

Ration Card No ...*415*... Date ...*6/3/90*

Valid upto ...*30-6-90*...

Name of Ration Card holder

Shri/Smti ...*Prem Dhan Chakma*...

Full address ...*Chakma*...
... ...*vill - I*... ... ...

Number of family members :—

Adult ...*2*... (in word) ...*(Two)*...

Minor ...*3*... (in word) ...*(Three)*...

Total ...*3½*... Unit ...*(Three half)*...

Name of F.P. Shop Name ...*Rekm*...
and location to which
this Ration Card Location ...*Rkm*...
is assigned.

Signature with seal designation
of issuing authority.

Annexure-IV: Copy of the order dated 31.12.1991 cancelling ration cards issued to Chakma in Arunachal Pradesh.

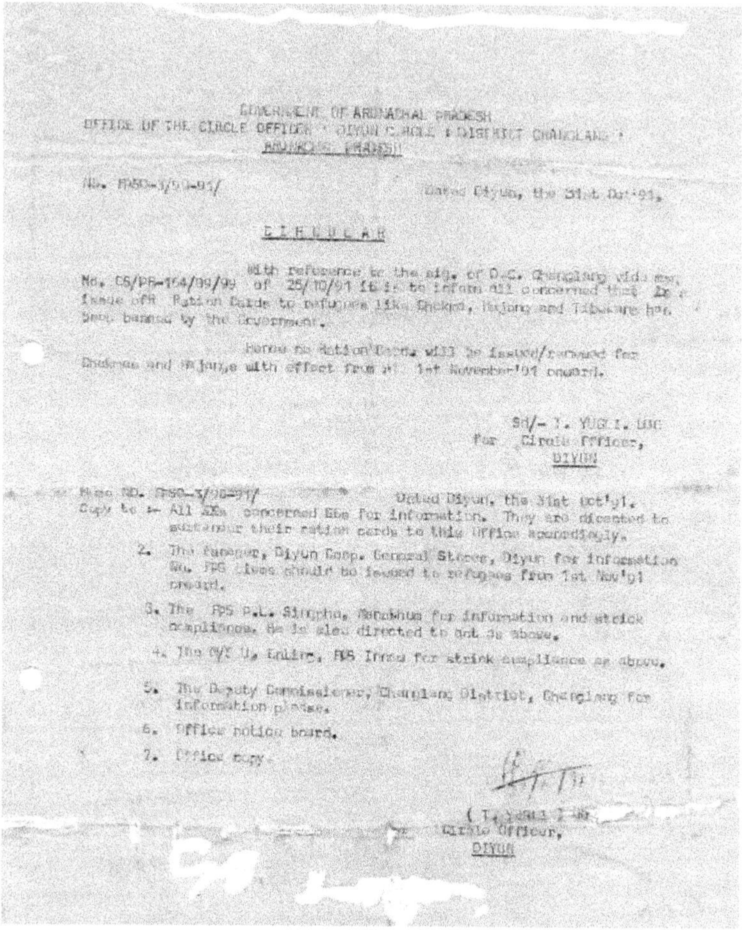

GOVERNMENT OF ARUNACHAL PRADESH
OFFICE OF THE CIRCLE OFFICER : DIYUN CIRCLE : DISTRICT CHANGLANG :
ARUNACHAL PRADESH

No. FPSO-3/50-91/   Dated Diyun, the 31st Oct'91.

CIRCULAR

With reference to the msg. of D.C. Changlang vide msg. No. CS/PR-164/90/99 of 25/10/91 it is to inform all concerned that the issue of Ration Cards to refugees like Chakma, Hajong and Tibetans has been banned by the Government.

Hence no Ration Cards will be issued/renewed for Chakmas and Hajongs with effect from 1st November'91 onward.

Sd/- T. YUGLI, UDC
for   Circle Officer,
DIYUN

Memo No. FPSO-3/50-91/   Dated Diyun, the 31st Oct'91.
Copy to :- All EACs concerned EOs for information. They are directed to surrender their ration cards to this Office accordingly.

2. The Manager, Diyun Coop. General Store, Diyun for information. No. FPS lines should be issued to refugees from 1st Nov'91 onward.

3. The FPS P.L. Singpho, Manakhua for information and strict compliance. He is also directed to act as above.

4. The CVT U. Enling, FPS Innao for strict compliance as above.

5. The Deputy Commissioner, Changlang District, Changlang for information please.

6. Office notice board.

7. Office copy.

(T. YUGLI)
Circle Officer,
DIYUN

Annexure-V: Copy of the Trade License issued to a Chakma individual on 23.05.1975.

GOVT. OF ARUNACHAL PRADESH
OFFICE OF THE DEPUTY COMMISSIONER: TIRAP DISTRICT;
KHONSA.
******

Trade Licence No. MIN/75 Dated Khonsa the 23-5-1975

Shri/Smti. KRISHNA KARBARI.

. . . . son/daughter/wife of Kali Kumar Karbari, an inhabitant of Sadipur village

is permitted to run a shop at Mahalihun .

sell the following items subject to the conditions prescribed below which he/she has accepted.

Type of shop to be run'   Annual fee to be paid
                                by the licence holder.

1. Grocery
2. Stationery
3. Cloth   C O N D I T I O N   Rs 100/- (hundred) received
                                           on 16.8.89.

The trade licence holder is to pay annual fee in advance against each category of items mentioned above for which he/she is authorised to deal with. The licence holder in normal course can engage two extra hand to run his/her business. But if he/she intended to engage more than two persons he/she will have to pay fee @ Rs. 5/-P.M. Rs. 2/- and Rs. 10/- for third, fourth and fifth additional hand respectively and in no case one permit holder be allowed to engage more than five persons his/her business.

shop and its surroundings will have to be kept clean all times.

No credit sale will be allowed to the local tribal and others, loan and advance also not to be given any one.

No excisable articles and liquor of any kind be sold in the shop.

No gambling be allowed.

He/she is to sell the articles at the rate by the rate board from time to time.

7.   He/she will not sublet his/her shop to any other persons.

8.   He/She will not sell any item except those category of articles mentioned in his/her licence.

9.   This permit shall remain valid for a calandar year and renewable on expiry, subject to the satisfactory performance in the past period.

Contd......P/2

175

Annexure-VI: Copy of the order dated 29.09.1980 prohibiting the appointment of Chakma and Hajongs in the State Government.

GOVERNMENT OF ARUNACHAL PRADESH – ITANAGAR

No.Pol-21/81   Dated the Itanagar 29th Sept/80

To

   The Deputy Commissioner
   Khonsa, Tirap Dist. (A.P.)

Sir,

   I am directed to refer to your letter
No. CA-103/78/75 dated 20/6/80 regarding employment
facilities to Chakmas/Hajongs/and other refugees under
the government. The matter is under examination and
therefore no appointment be given to Chakmas/Hajongs/Yobins
and Tibetan refugees till a final decision is arrived
at. Those who are already in govt. services may continue,
but should not be permanent.

   Further instruction in the matter will follow.

          Sd/-

         (B. Hussain)
        Secretary (Political)
         Itanagar

No.Pol-21/80 Dated Itanagar the 29th Sept/80

Copy to :-

   The all Deputy Commissioners/Adl. Deputy Commissioners
in Arunachal Pradesh.

          Sd/-

         (B. Hussain)
       Secretary (Political)
         Itanagar

Annexure-VII: Copy of the Election Card issued to a Chakma family during the First General Election in Arunachal Pradesh, 1978.

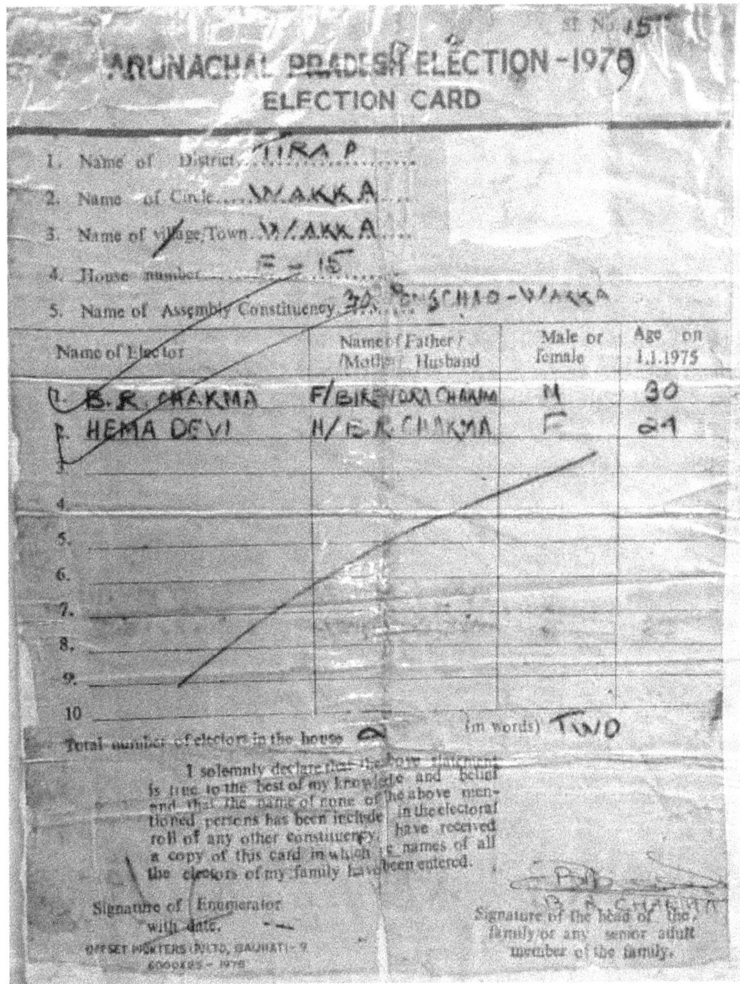

Name of Elector	Name of Father / Mother / Husband	Male or Female	Age on 1.1.1975
1. B. R. CHAKMA	F/ BIRENDRA CHAKMA	M	30
2. HEMA DEVI	H/ B. R. CHAKMA	F	24
3.			
4.			
5.			
6.			
7.			
8.			
9.			
10			

177

Annexure-VIII: Copy of the order dated 11.10.1994 cancelling the orders of appointment of Chakma and Hajong village authorities (Gaonburahs)

GOVERNMENT OF ARUNACHAL PRADESH
OFFICE OF THE DEPUTY COMMISSIONER
CHANGLANG DISTRICT:::CHANGLANG

NO. GA-3/GB/DYN/88/16045-63 Dated Changlang, the 11th Oct/94.

O R D E R

In exercise of powers under Section-3(1) of the Assam Frontier (Administrative of Justice) Regulations, 1945 (Regulation-1 of 1945) I, Shri A.K.Das, IAS, Deputy Commissioner, Changlang District hereby cancel the Orders of appointment as Village authority(GBs) of Changlang District in respect of the following persons as the appointees are not Indian citizens and are ineligible to exercise the powers of village authority under the Regulation.

1. Sri Sisir Kanti Dewan, GB, Bijoypur
2. Sri Surjyo Kumar Chakma, GB, Moitripur
3. Sri Kishore Kumar Dewan, Head GB, Gautampur
4. Sri Jitendra Lal Chakma, GB, Kamakhyapur
5. Sri Kripadhan Karbri, GB, Shantipur
6. Sri Surjyo Sen Chakma, GB, Jyotipur
7. Sri Prasanta Kumar Chakma, GB, Abhoypur
8. Sri Snaha Kumar Chakma, GB, Dumpathar
9. Sri Amrit Lal Chakma, GB, Udaipur
10. Sri Buddhu Lila Chakma, GB, Rajnagar
11. Sri Khudiram Chakma, GB, Joypur
12. Sri Mohendra Hazong, GB, Haripur
13. Sri Bichitra Hazong, GB, Srirampur
14. Sri Chitranjan Hazong, GB, Madhupur-I
15. Sri Dubaraj Hazong, GB, Madhupur-II
16. Sri Nilotpal Talukdar, Head GB Dumpani
17. Sri Shanti Kumar Chakma, GB, Jyotsnapur

The above mentioned persons shall cease to be a Village authority(GB) in Changlang District from the date of issue of this order.

Si/- (A.K.Das)IAS
Deputy Commissioner,
Changlang District,
Changlang.

Contd....2/-

178

Annexure-IX: Copy of the order dated 27.10.2022 cancelling the Residential Proof Certificates (RPC) to the Chakma and Hajong youths

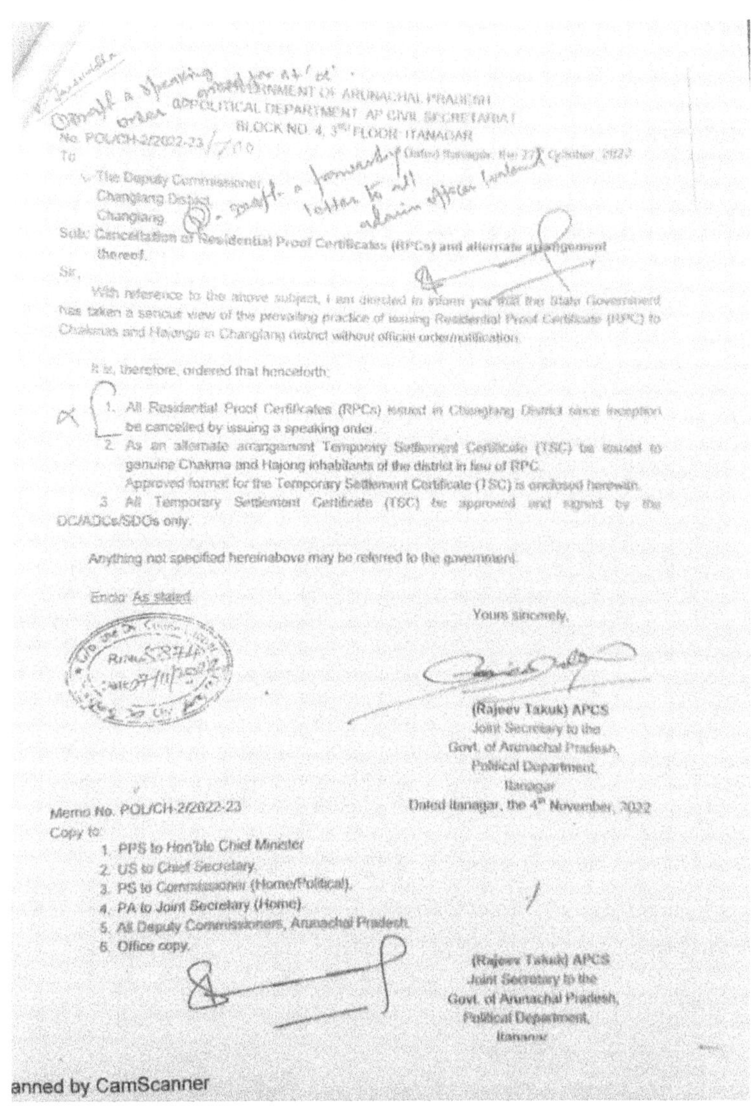

GOVERNMENT OF ARUNACHAL PRADESH
POLITICAL DEPARTMENT, AP CIVIL SECRETARIAT
BLOCK NO. 4, 3rd FLOOR, ITANAGAR

No. POL/CH-2/2022-23/700

Dated Itanagar, the 27th October, 2022

To

The Deputy Commissioner,
Changlang District
Changlang

Sub: Cancellation of Residential Proof Certificates (RPCs) and alternate arrangement thereof.

Sir,

With reference to the above subject, I am directed to inform you that the State Government has taken a serious view of the prevailing practice of issuing Residential Proof Certificate (RPC) to Chakmas and Hajongs in Changlang district without official order/notification.

It is, therefore, ordered that henceforth:

1. All Residential Proof Certificates (RPCs) issued in Changlang District since inception be cancelled by issuing a speaking order.

2. As an alternate arrangement Temporary Settlement Certificate (TSC) be issued to genuine Chakma and Hajong inhabitants of the district in lieu of RPC.
   Approved format for the Temporary Settlement Certificate (TSC) is enclosed herewith.

3. All Temporary Settlement Certificate (TSC) be approved and signed by the DC/ADCs/SDOs only.

Anything not specified hereinabove may be referred to the government.

Enclo: As stated

Yours sincerely,

(Rajeev Takuk) APCS
Joint Secretary to the
Govt. of Arunachal Pradesh,
Political Department,
Itanagar

Memo No. POL/CH-2/2022-23

Dated Itanagar, the 4th November, 2022

Copy to:

1. PPS to Hon'ble Chief Minister
2. US to Chief Secretary.
3. PS to Commissioner (Home/Political).
4. PA to Joint Secretary (Home).
5. All Deputy Commissioners, Arunachal Pradesh.
6. Office copy.

(Rajeev Takuk) APCS
Joint Secretary to the
Govt. of Arunachal Pradesh,
Political Department,
Itanagar

References

Reports and Documents

UNHCR, what is a refugee, https://www.unhcr.org/us/what-refugee

57 Years After India Gave Them Refuge, Former Refugees From East Pakistan Threatened By Indian Xenophobia |
Article-14, https://www.article-14.com/post/57-years-after-india-gave-them-refuge-former-refugees-from-east-pakistan-threatened-by-indian-xenophobia-61f9f4b18da1f

Ministry of Rehabilitation Letter No. 12/1/80-Desk.IV dated February 12, 1981, to the Govt. of Arunachal Pradesh (MHA File No. 13024/5/73 AP Vol. III), National Archives of India

Understanding the Indian Refugee Law Framework - https://nyaaya.org/guest-blog/understanding-the-indian-refugee-law-framework/

Refugees in India - Wikipedia, https://en.wikipedia.org/wiki/Refugees_in_India

Model National Law on Refugees - [2001] ISILYBIHRL 19, https://www.worldlii.org/int/journals/ISILYBIHRL/2001/19.html

India's Refugee Policy - Indian National Bar Association, https://www.indianbarassociation.org/indias-refugee-policy/

nluassam.ac.in, https://nluassam.ac.in/docs/Journals/NLUALR/Volume-7/Article%2011.pdf

Chakma of Arunachal Pradesh – CRDO, https://crdo.chakma.in/Chakma-of-arunachal-pradesh/

Statelessness : A Study of Chakma Refugees of Arunachal Pradesh - SAS Publishers,

https://www.saspublishers.com/article/4656/download/

land use pattern and food security of stateless: profile of arunachal Chakma, https://www.worldwidejournals.com/indian-journal-of-applied-research-(IJAR)/recent_issues_pdf/2019/October/land-use-pattern-and-food-security-of-stateless-profile-of-arunachal-Chakma_October_2019_1571897281_9711789.pdf

Chakma of Arunachal Pradesh – CRDO, https://crdo.chakma.in/Chakma-of-arunachal-pradesh/

The Tibetan Rehabilitation Policy, 2014. - Ministry of Home Affairs, https://www.mha.gov.in/sites/default/files/2022-08/FFR_ANNEXURE_A_17092019%5B1%5D.pdf

Chakma, Hajongs in Arunachal Pradesh Face 'Uncertain Future' l, https://www.smalegal.in/home/the-stateless-status-of-tibetans-in-india

Tibetan Refugees' Rights and Services in India - Digital Commons @ DU, https://digitalcommons.du.edu/cgi/viewcontent.cgi?article=1631&context=hrhw

Central Tibetan Relief Committee , https://www.nextias.com/ca/current-affairs/11-04-2022/central-tibetan-relief-committee

Chakma, Hajongs in Arunachal Pradesh Face 'Uncertain Future' as Government Plans Relocation - Land Conflict Watch, https://www.landconflictwatch.org/conflicts/Chakma-hajongs-in-arunachal-pradesh-face-uncertain-future-as-government-plans-relocation

https://www.indiacode.nic.in/bitstream/123456789/19895/1/the_right_to_fair_compensation_and_transparency_in_land_acquisition,_rehabilitation_and_resettlement_act,_2013..pdf

The Right to Fair Compensation and Transparency in Land Acquisition, Rehabilitation, and Resettlement Act, 2013 | O.P. Jindal Global University, https://jgu.edu.in/jsgp/jindal-policy-research-lab/the-right-to-fair-compensation-and-transparency-in-land-acquisition-rehabilitation-and-resettlement-act-2013/

Chakma of Arunachal Pradesh – CRDO, https://crdo.chakma.in/Chakma-of-arunachal-pradesh/

The Chakma-Hajong challenge - Observer Research Foundation, https://www.orfonline.org/expert-speak/chakma-hajong-challenge

land use pattern and food security of stateless: profile of arunachal Chakma, https://www.worldwidejournals.com/indian-journal-of-applied-research-(IJAR)/recent_issues_pdf/2019/October/land-use-pattern-and-food-security-of-stateless-profile-of-arunachal-Chakma_October_2019_1571897281_9711789.pdf

Chakma of Arunachal Pradesh – CRDO,
https://crdo.chakma.in/Chakma-of-arunachal-pradesh/

Chakma, Hajongs in Arunachal Pradesh Face 'Uncertain Future' as Government Plans Relocation - Land Conflict Watch,
https://www.landconflictwatch.org/conflicts/Chakma-hajongs-in-arunachal-pradesh-face-uncertain-future-as-government-plans-relocation

The Chakma-Hajong challenge - Observer Research Foundation,
https://www.orfonline.org/expert-speak/chakma-hajong-challenge

South Asia's Tibetan Refugee Community Is Shrinking, Imperiling Its Long-Term Future, https://www.migrationpolicy.org/article/tibetan-refugees-india

Freedom Fighters & Rehabilitation Division,
https://www.mha.gov.in/en/divisionofmha/freedom-fighters-rehabilitation-division

The Tibetan Rehabilitation Policy, 2014. - Ministry of Home Affairs,
https://www.mha.gov.in/sites/default/files/2022-08/FFR_ANNEXURE_A_170920190%5B1%5D.pdf

https://www.mha.gov.in/en/divisionofmha/freedom-fighters-rehabilitation-division

Office of the Registrar General & Census Commissioner, Ministry of Home Affairs, Government of India, https://new.census.gov.in/

MHA guidelines to State Governments regarding treatment of Minorities from East Pakistan, Letter No. 21/48/62-F. IV(B), File No. 13024/5/73-AP-II, Development and regulatory measures, Security matters - Settlement of Chakma Refugees in Arunachal Pradesh (National Archives of India)

Election Commission of India, Can a non-citizen of India become a voter in the electoral rolls in India? https://voters.eci.gov.in/HomePageFaq

Livelaw.in, which Documents Prove Indian Citizenship?,
https://www.livelaw.in/columns/which-documents-prove-indian-citizenship-153027

Tibetan Legal Association, Registration Certificate ,
https://tibetanlegalassociation.org/en/legal-overview-of-the-status-of-tibetans-in-india/

UNHCR, Refugee Status Determination,
https://help.unhcr.org/india/refugee-status-determination-2/

Section 5(1) in The Citizenship Act, 1955,
https://indiankanoon.org/doc/1860219/

Report Submitted by the Member Secretary, Aruanachal Pradesh State Legal Service Authority, Itanagar in Supreme Court Case WP(C) No. 510 of 2007, https://www.sci.gov.in/case-status-case-no/

The Citizenship Act, 1955, Citizenship by birth,
https://www.indiacode.nic.in/bitstream/123456789/6793/1/the_citizenship_act_1955.pdf

Electoral Roll, Arunachal Pradesh: https://ceoarunachal.nic.in/

Landmark Judgement on Election Law (A compilation of important Judgements prounced by the Supreme Court of India, High Courts and Election Commision of India, Volume-V) Delhi High Court WP (C) No. 886 of 2000, PUCL & CCRCAP vs Election Commission of India and PIL No. 52 of 2010 (AAPSU vs ECI)
https://ceodelhi.gov.in/WriteReadData/Landmark%20Judgments/LandmarkJudgementsVOLI.pdf

Government of India. (1955). The Citizenship Act, 1955.
https://legislative.gov.in/

National Human Rights Commission (NHRC). (n.d.). Reports on the Status of Chakma in Arunachal Pradesh. https://nhrc.nic.in/

Government of India. (2013). The National Food Security Act, 2013.
https://dfpd.gov.in/
Ministry of Minority Affairs. (n.d.). Pre-Matric and Post-Matric Scholarships for Minorities. https://minorityaffairs.gov.in/

Ministry of Health and Family Welfare. (n.d.). Pradhan Mantri Jan Arogya Yojana (PM-JAY). https://pmjay.gov.in/

Government of Arunachal Pradesh. (n.d.). Chief Minister Arogya
Arunachal Yojana (CMAAY). https://cmaay.com/

'Bhonti culture': How minor girls from Assam are sold into slavery in
Arunachal Pradesh by Maitreyee Boruah,
https://thefederal.com/category/the-eighth-column/bhonti-culture-how-
minor-girls-from-assam-are-sold-into-slavery-in-arunachal-pradesh-98342

The Core Idea – CRDO, https://crdo.chakma.in/crdo-the-core-idea/

What is Bengal Eastern Frontier Regulation in 1873,
https://eilp.arunachal.gov.in/actDetails

The Gauhati High Court, PIL No. 52 of 2010, Case Details:
https://hcservices.ecourts.gov.in

The National Archives of India – Ministry of Home Affairs File No.
13024/5/73AP Volume-III (Correspondence) Subject: Settlement of
Chakma in Arunachal Pradesh

M.M. Jacob, Minister of State for Home and Parliamentary Affairs, reply
letter to Laeta Umbrey, Member of Parliament,

Lok Sabha, D.O. No. 12/16/92-NE, 23 September 1992.

The National Archives of India – Ministry of Home Affairs NEFA
Section File No. NE/463(22) Subject: Visit of Members of Parliament to
NEFA in May 1966

The National Archives of India – Ministry of Home Affairs NEFA File
No. 13024/5/73-AP. II Subject: Settlement of Chakma Refugees in
Arunachal Pradesh

The National Archives of India – Ministry of Home Affairs NEFA File
No. 13024/5/73-AP. II Subject: Settlement of Chakma Refugees in
Arunachal Pradesh

Official Portal of Government of Tripura, Council of Ministers,
https://tripura.gov.in/council-ministers

Members for 9th Mizoram State Legislative Assembly,
http://mizoram.nic.in/gov/mla.htm

Executive Summary of the Report on 'The State of Being Stateless: A Case Study of the Chakma of Arunachal Pradesh' 1. 2025, http://www.mcrg.ac.in/statelessness.pdf

Deepak K. Singh, Stateless in South Asia: The Chakma between Bangladesh and India (New Delhi: SAGE Publications, 2010) https://www.researchgate.net/publication/360207455_Statelessness_A_Study_of_Chakma_Refugees_of_Arunachal_Pradesh

United Nations High Commissioner for Refugees (UNHCR), Definition of Stateless Persons, https://www.unhcr.org/ibelong/wp-content/uploads/1954-Convention-relating-to-the-Status-of-Stateless-Persons_ENG.pdf

Displaced, Denied, And Defiant: The Chakma's Fight for Citizenship, https://www.hinducollegegazette.com/post/displaced-denied-and-defiant-the-chakma-s-fight-for-citizenship-in-a-changing-india

CRDO: FAQ about Chakma, https://crdo.chakma.in/faqs-chakma-and-hajong-tribes-of-arunachal-pradesh-2/

The Chakma' Struggle for Citizenship: Breaking Down India's Citizenship Acquisition Regime, Moosa Izzat-NUJS Law Review 15 NUJS L. Rev. 3-4 (2022) https://nujslawreview.org/wp-content/uploads/2023/06/15.3-4.Izzat_.pdf

Displaced, Denied, And Defiant: The Chakma's Fight for Citizenship, https://www.hinducollegegazette.com/post/displaced-denied-and-defiant-the-chakma-s-fight-for-citizenship-in-a-changing-india

Arunachal: Chakma and Hajong Tribes Protest to Get Rid of the 'Refugee'Tag, https://www.newsclick.in/arunachal-chakma-and-hajong-tribes-protest-get-rid-refugee-tag

Why Chakma and Hajongs in Arunachal Pradesh are demanding their residence proof papers back, https://scroll.in/article/1041201/why-Chakma-and-hajongs-in-arunachal-pradesh-are-demanding-their-residence-proof-papers-back

Chakma, Hajong refugees to get Indian citizenship. All you need to know, https://www.indiatoday.in/india/story/chakma-hajong-refugee-indian-citizenship-1043986-2017-09-13

Open letter: Dear Rajnath Singh, the 'limited citizenship' for Chakma is too little, too late, Mahendra Chakma https://scroll.in/article/851111/open-letter-dear-rajnath-singh-the-limited-citizenship-for-Chakma-is-too-little-too-late

International Journal of Advance Research, IJOAR .org, Dr. Bindu Ranjan Chakma, https://archive.nyu.edu/bitstream/2451/44215/2/BETWEEN-AGONY-AND-HOPE-THE-CHAKMA-REFUGEES-OF-ARUNACHAL-PRADESH-OF-INDIA%20%281%29.pdf

A Question of Citizenship: The Case of the Chakma-Hajong Refugees - SPRF, Arunav Chetia, https://sprf.in/a-question-of-citizenship-the-case-of-the-chakma-hajong-refugees/

Article 16 in Constitution of India, Equality of opportunity in matters of public employment, https://indiankanoon.org/doc/211089/

The Arunachal Pradesh Panchayati Raj Act,1997, https://secap.nic.in/docs/Act/AP_PR_ACT.pdf

The Supreme Court of India, SLP (C) 14115 of 2022, Kali Ratan Chakma and Ors Vs State of Arunachal Pradesh and Ors. https://www.sci.gov.in/case-status-case-no/

The Gauhati High Court PIL No. 20 of 2017, https://hcservices.ecourts.gov.in/

The Government of Arunachal Pradesh Schemes, https://www.myscheme.gov.in/search/state/Arunachal%20Pradesh

Panchayati Raj Institutions (PRIs), https://www.nextias.com/blog/panchayati-raj-institutions/

Residential Proof Certificate revoked for Chakma and Hajongs, Order No. POL/CH-2/2022-23/100, Govt. of Aruanchal Pradesh, Political Department

Employment banned for Chakma and Hajongs in Arunachal Pradesh, Order No. Pol-21/81 29 Sep 1980

The Estimates Committee, Seventy-First Report (Third Lok Sabha) 1964-65, https://eparlib.nic.in/bitstream/123456789/4940/1/ec_3_82_1965.pdf

Interrogating Victimhood: East Bengali Refugee Narratives of Communal Violence Nilanjana Chatterjee Department of Anthropology - The Swadhinata Trust, https://swadhinata.org.uk/wp-content/uploads/2023/01/chatterjeeEastBengal-Refugee.pdf

Jely 18-25, 1964, http://web.stanford.edu/group/tomzgroup/pmwiki/uploads/1310-1962-xx-xx-KS-a-JZW.pdf

Partition of India and Migration from the Mymensing District of Erstwhile East Pakistan: A Study of Hajong Tribe - SAS Publishers, https://saspublishers.com/article/918/download/

P.N. Luthra, Adviser to the Governor of Assam to M.R. Yardi, Additional Secretary, Ministry of Home Affairs, New Delhi, D.O.No.RR.14/69, Shillong, the 10 April, 1969 (National Archives of India)

Negotiated Identity: A Study of Bangladeshi Migrants in Eastern India, https://www.tandfonline.com/doi/full/10.1080/15562948.2024.2416424?src=

Assam Accord - Supreme Court Observer, https://www.scobserver.in/cases/assam-sanmilita-mahshangha-union-of-india-assam-accord-case-background/

BENGALI REFUGEES, HUMAN RIGHTS AND THE ISSUE OF CITIZENSHIP IN EASTERN AND NORTH-EASTERN INDIA - Amazon S3, http://s3-ap-southeast-1.amazonaws.com/ijmer/pdf/volume10/volume10-issue8(3)/12.pdf
Ghotis and Bangals: Decoding a Very Bengali Rivalry, https://www.thequint.com/campaigns/bol/ghotis-and-bangals-decoding-a-very-bengali-rivalry

The Partition of Bengal & Assam - Bounday Report - Documents, https://www.partitionmuseum.org/partition-of-india/bengal-assam

1964 East Pakistan riots - Wikipedia, https://en.wikipedia.org/wiki/1964_East_Pakistan_riots

The Independence of Bangladesh in 1971 - The National Archives, https://www.nationalarchives.gov.uk/education/resources/the-independence-of-bangladesh-in-1971/

Partition of India and Migration from the Mymensing District of
Erstwhile East Pakistan: A Study of Hajong Tribe - SAS Publishers,
accessed April 5, 2025,
https://saspublishers.com/article/918/download/

Note Sent to the Deputy Secretary (NE), MHA, Govt. of India by R.K.
Patir, Commissioner cum Secretary (Home), Govt. of Arunachal Pradesh
on 31 May 1980, No. POL-57/79 (National Archives of India)

Tribes of North-East India: A Study on 'Hajongs', GJRA - GLOBAL
JOURNAL FOR RESEARCH ANALYSIS Volume : 3 | Issue : 2 | Feb
2014 • ISSN No 2277 - 8160,
https://www.worldwidejournals.com/global-journal-for-research-
analysis-GJRA/recent_issues_pdf/2014/February/tribes-of-north-east-
india-a-study-on-hajongs_February_2014_1598858860_83.pdf?

Hajong And Their Bastu Festival, IOSR Journal Of Humanities And
Social Science (IOSR-JHSS) Volume 28, Issue 5, Series 2 (May, 2023) 47-
50 e-ISSN: 2279-0837, p-ISSN: 2279-0845.
https://www.iosrjournals.org/iosr-jhss/papers/Vol.28-Issue5/Ser-
2/H2805024750.pdf

History of the Hajongs,
https://thehajongs.blogspot.com/2018/07/history-of-hajongs.html
Explained: The Hajong Tribe of Assam,
https://www.northeastbullet.com/hajong-tribe-of-assam/

Implementation of Assam Accord Department, Government of Assam,
https://assamaccord.assam.gov.in/portlets/the-assam-accord

Section 6A, Citizenship Act,1955, Special provisions as to citizenship of
persons covered by the Assam Accord.
https://www.indiacode.nic.in/show-
data?abv=CEN&statehandle=123456789/1362&actid=AC_CEN_5_40_
00001_195557_1517807319455§ionId=14352§ionno=6A&order
no=7&orgactid=AC_CEN_5_40_00001_195557_1517807319455

Constitutional History of Arunachal Pradesh,
https://appsc.gov.in/Index/history

THE NORTH-EASTERN AREAS (REORGANISATION) ACT, 1971,
https://www.indiacode.nic.in/bitstream/123456789/1534/1/197181.pdf

A Critical Analysis Of State Of Arunachal Pradesh V. Khudiram Chakma (AIR 1994 SC 1461) https://www.ijllr.com/post/a-critical-analysis-of-state-of-arunachal-pradesh-v-khudiram-chakma-air-1994-sc-1461

Ministry of Home Affairs, Indian Citizenship Online https://indiancitizenshiponline.nic.in/Documents/UserGuide/E-gazette_2019_20122019.pdf

Citizenship (Amendment) Act, 2019, Applicability of the Amended Act https://www.drishtiias.com/to-the-points/Paper2/citizenship-amendment-act-2019

District Census Hanbook Changlang https://censusindia.gov.in/nada/index.php/catalog/164/download/306/DH_2011_1209_PART_A_DCHB_CHANGLANG.pdf

Kamduk,J.(2016). Rise of Chakma Ethnic Consciousness in Arunachal Pradesh: An Instrumentalist approach. IOSR Journal of Humanities and Social Science (IOSRJHSS).21(5).24-29. www.iosrjournals.org

CRDO: What were the "at-par rights" enjoyed by the Chakma/Hajogns with other local tribal? https://crdo.chakma.in/faqs-chakma-and-hajong-tribes-of-arunachal-pradesh-2/

Chakma Society at the Crossroads: Unravelling Realities of Chakma Youths from Arunachal Pradesh | TICI Journal, Sintu Chakma, http://www.ticijournals.org/chakma-society-at-the-crossroads-unravelling-realities-of-chakma-youths-from-arunachal-pradesh/

NEFA-An Introduction: R.N. Haldipur

Claude Apri: The Indian Frontier Administrative Service: Romanticism and Hostile Borders, https://claudearpi.blogspot.com/2014/12/romanticism-and-hostile-borders.html

White Paper on Chakma and Hajong Refugee Issue, Govt. of Arunachal Pradesh, 1996

Ministry of Home Affairs, File No. 210(11)/63-NI, "Agricultural Settlement in NEFA: Model Schemes for Settlement and Correspondence Regarding Vijaynagar/Preetnagar Settlements" (National Archives of India).

Report of the Committee Formed to Examine Refugee Settlements in Arunachal Pradesh, Established by the Government of Arunachal Pradesh per Memo No. POL.236/72, dated December 8, 1976.

Press India Bureau, Weekly Digest of News, Vol.IX. No. 15 dated April 11, 1965

Rehabilitation of refugees and others in Assam including hill districts and North East Frontier Agency. MHA File No.   15/12/64-SR/R-A (National Archives of India)

Press India Bureau, Development Work Intensified in NEFA, April 4, 1965, https://archive.pib.gov.in/archive/ArchiveSecondPhase/EXTERNAL%20AFFAIRS/1965-APRIL-MAY-VOL-2-EXTERNAL-AFFAIRS/PDF/EXT-1965-04-04_036.pdf

Record of discussion held on June 22, 1965, between the Union Rehabilitation Minister and senior Assam officials, including the Rehabilitation Minister, Chief Secretary, and other state officers. (Assam Archives File)

Tour Note of H.S Butalia, Liaison Officer, Ministry of Rehabilitation, Govt. of India vide No. 13(23)/65-RH. I dated 19th July, 1965 regarding his visit to Goalpara and Garo Hills District and Tripura (Assam Archives File)

Development & Resettlement of of ex-services Sectors of the Indo Pakistan border and NEFA (217/16/65-NEFA) National Archives of India

Letter of Mr. P.N. Luthra, Adviser to the Governor of Assam vide No. D.O.R.R.14/69 dated 10th April 1969 to M.R. Yardi, Additional Secretary, Ministry of Home Affairs, New Delhi

ABOUT THE AUTHOR

Arunjit Chakma is a dedicated social activist from Diyun, Arunachal Pradesh, committed to advocating for the rights of the Chakma people. Holding a master's degree in English, he left a promising corporate career in Delhi in 2013 to focus on grassroots change for his community. Arunjit has held leadership roles in organizations like the Arunachal Pradesh Chakma Students Union (APCSU), Chakma National Council of India (CNCI-AP), and Chakma Rights and Development Organization (CRDO).

Following his first book, *The Chakma of Arunachal Pradesh: History, Challenges and Aspirations*, this is his second work addressing the Chakma and Hajong issues in Arunachal Pradesh. His journey inspires young leaders to drive meaningful societal impact.